CONTENTS

JAMES C. SCHAAP

DON'T PRAY WITH MUD ON YOUR SHOES

CRC Publications
Grand Rapids, Michigan

Text illustrations: Paul Stoub

Schaap, James C., 1948-
Don't pray with mud on your shoes / James C. Schaap.
p. cm. — (Devotions for today)
Summary: A collection of forty-five meditations on the book of Numbers, a continuation of the Exodus story.
ISBN 1-56212-123-5
1. Bible. O.T. Numbers I-XX—Devotional literature.
2. Teenagers—Prayer-books and devotions—English. [1. Bible. O.T. Numbers.
2. Prayer books and devotions. 3. Christian life.] I. Title. II. Series.
BS1565.4.S33 1995
222'.1406—DC20 95-32211
CIP
AC

10 9 8 7 6 5 4 3 2 1

PREFACE

Numbers is one of those Old Testament books that often goes largely unread. Unless you are doggedly plodding through every chapter and verse in the Bible from Genesis to Revelation, this is an easy book to skip over in your devotional reading. It begins with a detailed census of the people of Israel, followed by various rites of purity, kinds of offerings, and rules about the tabernacle. Not much of interest here, you may suppose.

In *Don't Pray with Mud on Your Shoes,* author James C. Schaap will show you differently. Schaap takes the first twenty chapters of the book of Numbers and demonstrates the living dialogue that occurs between God and God's people. For instance, regarding the Lord's demand (3:46-47) of five shekels for each of the 273 extra firstborn Israelites, Schaap writes:

> *Let's face it. God doesn't need a piddly 1,365 extra shekels. He's got the whole world in his hands.*
>
> *But he wants us not to forget—not Moses or the Israelites or his people today . . . [that] there's a price for redemption. . . . He wants us only to remember who paid the biggest bill of all time.*

James C. Schaap is a professor of English at Dordt College in Sioux Center, Iowa. He has written two earlier books in this *Devotions for Today* series dealing with the dramatic trek of the Israelites from Egypt to Palestine: *100% Chance of Frogs* and *The 40-Year Campout.*

Teens and their families will enjoy using this book for devotional reading. We offer it with the conviction that readers will gain a deeper appreciation of this book of the Bible and a deeper understanding of God's gracious dealings with the Israelites and with us.

Harvey A. Smit
Editor in chief
Education, Worship, and Evangelism Department
CRC Publications

MEDITATION 1

G-MAIL

Read Numbers 1:1.

Back in the olden days, I used to write books by hand. It's hard to believe I ever got along without this electronic brain-box in front of me, but I used to use a pen, a long thing packing a little vial of ink in the skinniest of tubes. You'd drag its end over paper and a line would appear—ask your grandparents.

I used to sit at a desk and write stories—"draw" them out, because each letter of each word had to be done separately. (Please, your mouth is gaping.)

Of course, in the olden days, snowbanks rose as high as telephone wires, and I walked twenty-seven miles—one way—to school each day, while Ma baked bread every day from scratch. . . .

But right now, I'm sitting in our basement staring into the blue screen of my Apple IIGS (I know, it's a dinosaur), and the only sound in the room is the ticking of plastic keys beneath my fingers. (I take that back, our dehumidifier is whirring.)

I'm writing on a computer because it's made the job of writing, of passing on information, much, much easier. Some people claim we live in an "information age," a time when the most significant operation in our society is the ability to transfer information from my place to yours with blinding speed.

I've got a confession to make—I'm a mail junkie. I've been addicted to watching my mail for years. Every summer day, I go to my office at school just to check my mail.

But this year I've got two other information sources to check—both electronic: an answering machine hooked up to my telephone, and E-mail, the flashiest means of getting mail I know of. I type a letter on my school computer, hit a few keys, and zap!—my letter slaps up on the computer screen of my old friend in Michigan. Pow, I'm there. E-mail.

We're about to read big chunks of the book of Numbers. One of this book's most distinguishing features is the fact that the phrase "The LORD spoke to Moses" occurs eighty-five times! Lots of info being passed along. Lots of communication.

I don't know how God spoke, but maybe it was like E-mail. In the movie *The Ten Commandments*, Moses stands by as God uses something like a laser to burn the Ten Commandments onto stone slate. Those were great special effects, but I don't think God picked up that kind of pen every time he wanted to direct Moses during the Israelite's wasteland wanderings.

Of course, God communicates in other ways. Some people *see* his glory in mountain streams, in prairie vistas, in meadows undulating with wildflowers, in a city skyline, in baby kittens, or in the wonderful pageant of colors in pigeon feathers. God doesn't pop out of old bottles, genie-like, although he could if he wanted to.

I like to think that the way God spoke to Moses was like E-mail because it seems that Moses, quite simply, got zapped with the information he needed. Suddenly, he knew. What God wanted appeared on the computer screen of his mind. God-mail. In the blink of an eye.

The tragedy is, however, that Moses didn't always get the message—which is not to say he didn't hear it. Truckers, who have their own CB language, might describe it this way: Moses didn't always have his ears on.

We may be amazed that Moses didn't always "get it" when God spoke to him. But then, neither do we. Sometimes it's much easier to believe what appears on our computer screens than what we hear from God almighty.

But that's only part of the story. Stay tuned. More info coming.

Lord, help us to hear your voice in our everyday lives. Grant us the ability to know your will as Moses knew your voice. Open our eyes, Lord, help us to see Jesus. Amen.

MEDITATION 2

THE SWARM

Read Numbers 1:17-22, 44-46.

In the NBA finals a couple of years ago, the invincible Michael Jordan led the Chicago Bulls to what everybody called a "threepeat," their third consecutive basketball championship.

Big deal. Here in Iowa, where I live, Jordan, Scotty Pippen, Horace Grant, and all the other Bulls couldn't tie the shoelaces of our team—the big, bad Iowa Hawkeyes. Yeah, in your face and all of that. We're talking bad here—big **BAD** Hawkeyes.

Okay, okay. Last year they were bad. In football, at least, they stunk worse than their shoes. Chosen to run for the Big Ten championship with Michigan, they flopped. The whole state wept. Season tickets are down this year.

But my word, did they *look* mean. The Hawks have this great way of coming out on the field. It's called "the swarm." First they huddle in close to each other, so close their knees almost butt the guys in front of them.

Then they jog—really, really slow. They don't run onto the field like every other two-bit football team; shoot, dogs can run. When the Hawks take the field, they swarm. Listen, they come on like a plague of monsters, an amoeba of muscle.

Last year they didn't play as tough as they looked. But soon enough we'll be starting another football season. When we do, mark my words: Beware the swarming Hawks. Maybe.

I don't think the Hawks's coach picked up the trick from the Israelites, but think about the swarm of Jewish folks that came together in the desert once they shook Pharaoh off in the Red Sea.

Just exactly how many of them there were is a question Bible scholars can bicker about forever. But we know this: if the word Moses himself used to describe the number—*elaph*—a word my Bible translates to mean "thousand"—really means a thousand in number, then the Israelite swarm was two million—a multitude the size of, say, Washington D.C. or Montreal.

Now I don't want to break down anybody's faith, but on some specifics, the Bible, as we read it, isn't perfectly reliable. Sometimes word meanings change. If I were to call my wife a *gossip,* for instance, she'd likely retaliate in some unseemly fashion, even though the word *gossip* once meant someone close to God. Besides, she's not a gossip—the chatty kind, at least.

Many people who study the Bible very closely think that the same kind of change in meaning occurred to the word *elaph*. Once, long before anybody remembers, that word may have meant "family" or "clan." Or it might have meant something like "troop," since the numbers being counted in this long passage seem to refer primarily to fighting men.

Two million people, plus all their flocks, camping out in the desert seems just a bit much. But whether there were two million or twenty thousand, a figure some claim to be more accurate, keeping that kind of wandering swarm together was no picnic.

Maybe that's why Numbers begins with a census. The Lord told Moses to get a handle on this swarm, to bring this multitude into line. After all, what they faced was a whole lot more than a football game. The Canaanites would be no pushover, and Israel had to do a lot more than look good. A people who for too long had been nothing more than slaves now had miles and miles to go. They couldn't do it as a swarm.

When we think of how difficult it must have been for so many people to begin a long trek into the desert, we can't help but reflect on your love for them, Lord. You are a God who serves your people, who loves them—who loves us. Thank you for your promises, Lord. Amen.

MEDITATION 3

MY DAUGHTER, THE FUNERAL DIRECTOR

Read Numbers 1:47-54.

My daughter Andrea recently took one of those tests designed to reveal what she should do with her life. You know the type: "Would you rather throw a javelin or teach a parakeet to speak Swahili?" Answer a whole booklet full of those questions and you'll realize your destiny.

The results were odd: according to the test she should think about becoming either a salesman of agricultural products (like me, she doesn't know a rotary hoe from a spring-tooth plow), or, of all things, a funeral director.

Now Andrea would rather pull my last month's socks out of a clothes hamper than get any kind of inoculation from a doctor. The thought of hypodermic needles makes her teeth bleed. So neither her mother nor I could begin to imagine our daughter someday performing whatever rituals go on in the back parlors of funeral homes. Her results got mixed up with someone else's, we assumed.

Sometime later, I was asked to be an "honorary pallbearer" at a funeral. I wasn't sure what that meant, but I found out. This funeral wasn't terribly sad; the death brought an end to long-term suffering. Everyone thought about the deceased, but no one did much weeping.

When it was over, the funeral director told the honorary pallbearers to exit the chapel before the honest-to-goodness pallbearers, who toted the casket. Once we were outside, the funeral director looked at me and whispered (there was absolutely no one around to hear him—I'm not sure why he whispered), "Honorary pallbearers stand at the edge of the rug." (They'd laid a special rug down on the sidewalk.) So we did. We took orders.

The casket was brought to the hearse, and the funeral director once more whispered to me, "Honorary pallbearers stand at the left back fender," as if all of these instructions were some municipal code.

Then it occurred to me that Andrea's test wasn't far off the mark. Funeral Director. What this guy was doing was structuring the details of an important event—making sure we knew our roles, even if those instructions seemed odd both to me and the rest of the honorary pallbearers.

My daughter loves planning things. She said yesterday that there were only thirty-six hours left until the pictures from her recent trip to Washington, D.C., would be ready to pick up at Wal-Mart. She loves putting things together, planning, structuring. Someday, she should make the kind of hostess who can throw unforgettable galas.

All of the rigmarole of the first chapter of Numbers is really about organization, control, a means by which to turn this swarm of Israelites into a disciplined nation. After eleven of the twelve tribes were counted, the Levites received their special instructions—they were to be in charge of the tabernacle. That was no small task. Wherever they went in the wilderness, the tabernacle had to go. Think of the logistics!—the packing, the unpacking, the setting up and the breaking down. The Levites were in charge of all the goods of worship. They were to be the planners, the funeral directors. With such a mass of folks on the hoof in the wilderness, everyone had to have a job. This swarm had to know its separate functions.

God appointed Moses to be the great funeral director in charge of all the planning. And as the Israelites begin their trek, it was important that everyone's nose be counted, everyone's job outlined clearly.

Administration. Strategic planning. These were very important to the swarm of Israelites.

Lord, grant us the patience to see the little things of our lives as you do. May we see every moment and every action, every morning and every evening, as yours. Thank you for your love for every single part of our lives. Amen.

MEDITATION 4

LOGISTICS

Read Numbers 2:1-18.

Just a few years ago, the town I live in turned into a carnival. Every year, the state's biggest newspaper sponsors a bike trip that takes people on a sometimes squiggly path from the western boundary of the state of Iowa all the way to the Mississippi on the east—well over five hundred miles.

This event—called RAGBRAI (the *Register*'s Annual Great Bike Ride Across Iowa)—attracts of tons of people, more than ten thousand, in fact. City people might not think of thirteen thousand as much of a crowd; but try to guess, just for starters, how many extra porta-potties a town like this one—population five thousand—has to set up to accommodate three times as many people as ordinarily flush in a single day.

Think of the extra beds. Think of the extra food. Actually, lots of people thought so much about the extra food that when RAGBRAI came to Sioux Center, every church and school organization set up some kind of food stand—brats to burgers to boiled potatoes with your favorite toppings. Not everything sold. Some people are still eating leftovers.

For a single night, Sioux Center, Iowa, became bed-and-breakfast host to thousands of extra people. The place really rocked. But it took incredible planning to take care of *logistics*, setting up for the bare essentials.

No matter exactly how many Israelites there were post-exodus, we know there was a swarm of folks following up on a promise made long ago, traveling some unknown path to the promised land. But Moses had to face the problem of logistics—how on earth is all of this going to work? Where are we going to wash our dishes?

Chapter 2 takes up where chapter 1 left off—more logistics. The tribes of Israel are assigned their camping sites: Judah to the east, Issachar and Zebulun beside them; Reuben to the south, along with Simeon and Gad; on the west side, Ephraim, Manasseh and Benjamin; the tribes of Dan, Asher, and Naphtali to the north.

Smack dab in the middle was the spot reserved for the Tent of Meeting, and the custodians thereof—the tribe of Levi. Why? Well, what's in the middle is most protected, of course. If you've ever seen any old Westerns, you know what it means to "circle the wagons"—draw a protective circle around what you treasure most. Of course, this plan wasn't Moses' design. God told him: this is the way it should be—I AM in the middle.

But God's story in Exodus is really a story of definition. What God did to Pharaoh, he still does for us when we read that story—he defines himself as the *only* true God. The Egyptians had more gods than Wisconsin has dairies. But they learned there was only one.

And this one isn't just some image of hard clay. What separated this Tent of Meetings from the temples erected to thousands of Mesopotamian gods was that in this tabernacle there would be *no* graven image. No human being could create a dummy with the stature of this incredible ruler of heaven and earth—that's number one of the commandments Moses hand-delivered from Sinai. This God—the God of deliverance, the God of the fertile Nile and the God of arid desert—was, and is, the real thing.

What Moses faced—and he'd seen it already the time he'd come down from the mountain—was a mob. What God wanted was order, discipline, structure. All of that started at the very center of the encampment, in the Tent of Meetings. God wanted himself there, in the very heart of his people.

Still does. Nothing's changed.

In all our busyness, Lord, in the stress that accumulates in our lives because we're always on the go, help us to keep you in the very center of our lives. Help us put up the Tent of Meeting at the very center of every last thing we do. Amen.

MEDITATION 5

GOD'S JUSTICE

Read Numbers 3:1-4; Leviticus 10:1-3.

Some mornings, as I left for my high school teaching job years ago, I'd tell my wife that some kid in my class was, that day, going to die.

Now I never killed anybody when I was teaching in high school. What I meant was that some kid was going to catch a full dose of my own brand of home-brewed unholy wrath.

Teaching can be fun—sometimes. But when the whole class is sky-high because of a big game or a faculty pie-eating contest or Sadie Hawkins Day, teaching can be an endless horror. On those days nobody cares about Ralph Waldo Emerson.

Some days at 4:00, I knew that unless I got tough the next day, the whole crazy classroom would be bananas—twenty-five kids doing nonstop, high-intensity blabbering. Some days I knew I would have to scream to get attention. It didn't matter who triggered the storm, somebody was going to catch it. A two-by-four up-side the head, some people call it.

"Dad," my daughter might say, "that's not fair." And she's right.

Take Edmund, a kid with an earring and a few measly whiskers. Most of the semester he's been okay—a little daydreaming and too much yapping when he was putting a move on Sally in the tank top. But Edmund's no criminal—not really.

One day, though, he comes into class and RIGHT IN THE MIDDLE OF MY GREAT LECTURE ON SHAKESPEARE, leans over backwards to try to light up sassy Sally.

Suddenly—and innocently, he stares up at an overweight teacher with bleeding fangs, who threatens to core poor Edmund's Adam's apple in a fascinating ritual right there in front of the whole world—oral surgery.

"But Mr. Schaap," Edmund says, "I didn't do nothing [double negative] I didn't do all semester long."

Makes no difference to me. That day I knew it was time to unload. It didn't make any difference whether it was Edmund or lowly LouElla or the peacock Pierre. It was time to take back the classroom.

Not fair? My daughter's right. It wasn't fair. "You *used* Edmund, really, didn't you, Dad—for the rest of the class?"

I admit it—I did. And it wasn't fair.

In today's passage, Aaron's boys, Nadab and Abihu, nice boys from the temple, brewed up a fire God didn't specifically design. Then tried to peddle their little creation as something that carried God's own signature.

Pardon the language, but the Lord unloaded. They were killed.

My daughter would say—and so might I, in fact—that such an incredibly difficult punishment wasn't fair to poor Nadab and Abihu. Death for one tiny lie?

In Acts, Ananias and Sapphira were struck dead for fibbing about finances. And in 2 Samuel, Uzzah fell like an oak for trying to keep the Ark of the Covenant from slipping off a wagon. In Joshua, Achan, who was dazzled by the Babylonian jewelry streaming through his fingers, got himself stoned by the whole Israeli clan for pocketing the goods. In each of those cases, it seems, God wanted to impress everybody else with how seriously he takes this matter of obedience.

There's a pattern here—God setting out rules for new communities not only by law, but by very graphic example.

Is it fair? I don't know.

But, really, what does God know about fair? He condemned his own son to death for our sakes. That wasn't *fair* to his son, was it?

God's standards of fair are not mine or my daughter's—and they're not the United Nations'. They're his. They're divine.

Abihu and Nadab ended up looking death in the face a lot earlier than they'd ever guessed they might. And all of Israel got the picture. Do you see it?

Stories like these, Lord, are not so easy to take. We like to think of you as someone who cares—and you do. But you are righteous, God, and you demand our obedience. Thank you for showing us your power. Amen.

MEDITATION 6

DESTINY

Read Numbers 3:5-14.

In the last few games of the NBA finals a few years ago, it seemed the Phoenix Suns were doomed. However, Charles Barkley, who plays even better than he talks, kept spouting off about the Suns' winning despite the odds, because it was, he said, "our destiny."

People don't often use the word *destiny,* so I perked up my ears. Barkley claimed he told Michael Jordan the same thing. "I told him it was our *destiny!*" he told reporters. He said Jordan laughed.

Michael might have laughed because he knew the Bulls were going to win, but he must have had to chuckle too, just like the rest of us, because Barkley's talk about *destiny* is plain weird. If he had turned out to be right, people would have said that Sir Charles was a prophet, a holy man, because *destiny,* in most people's minds, has to do with supernatural powers.

Phoenix lost. Barkley should stick to hanging from rims; he's clearly no great shakes at reading crystal balls.

Destiny. What a heavy word. When I read today's passage, I think of the destiny of some little Levite boy born into a clan where every last boy became a temple worker. Had to. No choice.

That's un-American, isn't it? A friend of mine, born in Europe, came to Canada in part because he was told in the country he left that he could not go to the university; he wasn't smart enough. Today, he's a world-class researcher in computers and microwaves.

Now imagine a boy named Joash, born into a nice Levite family—good parents, middle-class income, decent little tent, maybe even a pair of fine spotted donkeys. But here's the downer: the moment Joash is born, his destiny is to become a temple custodian.

He's got no choices. If he goes off to music camp, falls for the sousaphone, and dreams of a career with an orchestra, that's tough. If he wants to run for public office, he can't. Even if he's got Kirby Puckett's sweet swing, baseball is out of the question. Joash the Levite's destiny is set—as all destinies are—forever.

I'm American, through and through. To me, it seems like something a dirty rotten scoundrel communist might create. Where's the kid's freedom, after all? Shouldn't every last one of us be free to be what we can be? Follow your dream! How many Disney tunes don't have a line like that? You can be what you want to be.

Not in the Old Testament. God says, "The Levites are mine." He didn't ask, didn't even break it to them gently. Just pointed. "I let you Israelites live through the death of all the firstborn, and now that tribe," he says, pointing at the Levites, "are *mine*."

Sometimes the Lord God of Hosts is purely un-American.

But take my Canadian friend—do you think it's accurate to say that he is where he is today simply because of his own hard work? Do you think that maybe God had something to do with the fact that he immigrated to Canada, that there was enough money for him to go to the University of Alberta, that his mind works quickly, that he loves math and science? Did all of those things just happen? Was it all a matter of a little luck and his own hard work and determination?

Somehow I doubt it. What God wants, he gets. He's the King—was in the Old Testament, and still is. *You're mine,* he told the Levites.

They were. And so are we.

Lord, thank you for making us your family, for marking us as your people, for giving us a destiny that includes a past and a present and a future in your hand. Give us the strength to see, from day to day, that all our moments and movements are really yours. Amen.

MEDITATION 7

GOOD SENSE / GOD SENSE / GOD'S CENTS

Read Numbers 3:40-51.

I'm sorry. I'm not trying to be disrespectful. I know the Bible is the Word of God—the Lord's own account of his dealings with his people. But this stuff sometimes leaves me in a sea-fog haze.

Like today's passage. God tells Moses to count the firstborn Israelites. I'm not sure how Moses did that—whether he counted only the firstborn of each father, or only the firstborn of a mother (Israelite husbands had as many wives as today's husbands have golf clubs), or whether he had some other formula.

What we do know is that Moses has to count noses because the Lord wants him to figure out his bill—and that's where things start getting odd.

For every firstborn Israelite male, God says, he takes a Levite—one for one. For every Jewish boy saved from death during the Jews' last awful night in Egypt, the Lord gets a Levite. Why? Simple. "I'm the Lord—that's why." End of discussion.

So Moses takes out his chalk and starts scratching marks on the side of his tent. The number he tallies is 22,273—precisely 273 more Israelite firstborn than the total number of Levites. In other words, the Jews still have an outstanding bill; they owe the Lord for exactly 273 firstborn who were redeemed the night of the first Passover. How are they going to pay?

No problem. Verse 47 says that Moses was to collect five shekels for each of those extra 273 and give the money to Aaron and his sons, the temple custodians. Precisely in that way, Israel would pay off what it owed.

What I want to know is this—is the Lord God Almighty in this for the dough or what? I thought the miraculous thing about redemption, about grace itself, is that it's free. I can't buy my way into heaven in the same way I can buy life insurance, right?

So what's the deal here? This passage makes God sound like some tightfisted landlord. "By the way," he says, "you like the way my angels swept through Egypt that night and turned that jackal Pharaoh's hard heart into mush? You saw how easily I did that, did you? You saw those hoards dog-paddle through the Red Sea? You like that? Well, guess what. You owe me."

Sounds crass. An extra 273 Israeli firstborn, at five shekels a nose? Let me figure here—that comes to 1,365 shekels. I'm the Lord. Pay up.

But if my son comes to me on Monday asking for a pool table, Tuesday aching for a season ticket to the Kansas City Royals, Wednesday dying for a backyard swimming pool, Thursday a new TV—and so forth through the next two weeks—I know this: I'd better not give him everything. Even if I have the money, if I give him every last thing his heart desires, I'll spoil him rotten. *Spoil* is the right word—ever gulp spoiled milk?

Let's face it. God doesn't need a piddly 1,365 extra shekels. He's got the whole world in his hands.

But he wants us not to forget—not Moses or the Israelites or his people today either, whether they're in St. Louis, St. Catharines, St. Paul, or St. Croix. He wants us to know there's a price for redemption.

He doesn't really need our shekels. He wants us only to remember who paid the biggest bill of all time. So don't forget.

Forgive our forgetfulness, Lord. What our minds often lose track of is the cost of our own redemption. We take that far too casually sometimes, Lord. Help us to keep track of the cost of your suffering. Amen.

MEDITATION 8

HOLY THINGS

Read Numbers 4:1-14.

There's a desk in Mickey's room at home, an old desk. It's got a dozen little compartments full of baseball cards, class pictures, track ribbons, and old coupons he never uses but never throws away.

Inside one of those cubbyholes is a crumpled Kleenex—actually it seems a little gross. He ought to throw it away. But he doesn't.

Mickey is no pig. All right, maybe his room isn't the cleanest in the neighborhood, but it's not hopeless. There are T-shirts on the floor and maybe six caps flopped in the corners—only two on the rack his mother bought him.

Mickey's not a slob. He's normal. He goes to college—his first year—and he lives at home, studies at that desk almost every night. Even though he doesn't take it out, he knows very well that the crumpled-up Kleenex is third cubbyhole from the left, top row.

You see, Mickey's girlfriend, Kris, is in Illinois at college, the same school where her parents went to school "a century ago," she says. That college gave her a music scholarship, and she was anxious to get away from home—which is not to say she didn't like her parents. She just wanted to get away. That's understandable.

When she first left, Mickey got a letter every day. Then, every other day, then twice a week. It's December, a week before Christmas vacation, and he's not seen a letter in two weeks. He lives in Seattle, by the way; Kris doesn't get home on weekends.

That crumpled Kleenex doesn't get thrown out because somewhere inside—even though now it's completely dry—are Kris's tears from the night she left for college. They were sitting in his car, outside her house, the night before she flew to Chicago. She cried, and he held her softly, kept giving her Kleenex. He cried too.

The next morning, she was gone and his car was strewn with balled-up Kleenex. He threw them all out—except one, the one that now is stuffed in the cubbyhole of his desk, the one he knows is there, even if he doesn't uncrumple it or look at it, even if he only glances at it occasionally.

To him, it's almost a holy thing. Nobody in the whole world knows about it. It's tucked far enough back into that cubbyhole so his mother won't simply chuck it sometime when she's picking up his room. Nobody on earth knows that it almost magically holds the emotions they felt that last night. Only he knows.

But he also knows that in his case, absence didn't make the heart grow fonder. And he knows that he's losing Kris. When she comes back to Seattle next week, there'll be a difference because he's not been there to notice all the changes that have happened to her in Chicago, living so far away from her parents, so far away from him.

But he's still got hope. All semester long, he's been waiting for her. In the back of his mind, his whole future is already staked out. She's going to transfer back to some college in Washington next year; they'll be married. Kris doesn't exactly know that, but in Mickey's mind it's a done thing. But he's scared. At least he's got that Kleenex. Sometimes he takes it out and holds it in his hand.

So if you're ever in his room, take a glance at that desk—if it's open. Third cubbyhole from the left. Don't touch it though. That Kleenex doesn't have a thing to do with church, but to him it's a holy thing.

Dear Lord, help us to respect each other—and ourselves too—for we know that we are your holy things. Help us to care. Amen.

MEDITATION 9

CLEANLINESS AND GODLINESS

Read Numbers 5:1-4.

A couple of minutes ago, I walked out to our postage-stamp-size garden, pulled out a few weeds, and uprooted some tiny trees sprouting from the whirlybird seeds our old maple sends afluttering each spring. Our house doesn't need painting—not yet really. The lawn is mowed, the hedges trimmed. If some neighbor were to drive by—as they do—they'd certainly say the Schaaps keep a neat place.

In his book *God Talk,* Randy Vander Mey claims that when people in a small town like the one I live in advise a brand-new neighbor that they just love keeping their yards clean, it's really a warning: so should the new neighbor. Vander Mey is right. This town prides itself on cleanliness. (Maybe it's time I edge my lawn.) "Cleanliness is next to godliness" is one of those little precepts so deeply ingrained in us that I could find folks here who believe the line is divinely inspired and parked somewhere in the book of Hezekiah.

The Israelites were even more uptight about cleanliness. The passage for today makes another one of those judgments that makes us shudder. God commands Moses to tell the people that those who have specific ailments simply have to leave. There's no mainstreaming among the wandering Israelites: You got a rash, dear—you're out of the parade. Often as not, the Israelites associated disease on the skin with disease beneath it—disease in the soul. Smells like discrimination to me!

I like my dentist, but I hate what he does to me. Not long ago, I had a horrible toothache—in fact, it had grown into a headache by the time I finally went in (that's how much I hate to sit in a dentist's chair). What I needed, he said, was a root canal.

So he drilled into the root of the infected tooth, cleaned out the ugliness that was creating the pain, then sealed the whole thing up and put a cap on it. Now my tooth is sealed and dead—but so is the pain.

I asked the dentist what would have happened to me if I was out here on the plains, say, in 1830, when there wasn't a dentist between here and Fort Carson, and the only way of dealing with a toothache was a pair of pliers, a bottle of moonshine, and some heavy grunting.

"If you didn't get it, the infection would grow," he said.

"Then?" I asked.

"Probably—eventually—you'd just die."

Die of a toothache? Imagine that. "Jonas Buchanan, old trapper, buckskin man, veteran of the Indian wars, died today, downtown Sioux Center, of a toothache." Unbelievable.

The thing to remember when reading passages like this, thick with attitudes we find uncomfortable today, is that the Israelites didn't own a subscription to the *New England Journal of Medicine*. They didn't know a whole lot about health and disease. Moses was a wise man, but he couldn't do a root canal. Along the old Canaan trail, people died fast.

To the Israelites, cleanliness *was* godliness. They were a wandering swarm in a hostile environment, and their number-one priority wasn't facelifts or liposuction. Plain and simple, it was survival.

Here in Sioux Center, all I have to do is keep my weeds down and I can get along. Life in the wilderness was nowhere near as pillow-soft. Disease could wipe out half the camp before mid-morning lunch, so they had to take precautions. We have to remember, it was a whole different world.

Excuse me. Tomorrow's Sunday. I better wash the car.

Lord, only you can make us clean. Help us not to judge others, and judge us only by your love. Amen.

MEDITATION 10

RESTITUTION

Read Numbers 5:5-10; Psalm 51.

Let's face it. Even though the Bible doesn't carry parental warnings, the way some contemporary music does, it has more than a few R-rated stories.

For pure unmitigated violence, just think of King David *smiting* (there's an Old Testament word) eighteen thousand Edomites in the Valley of Salt. For flat-out horrifying treachery, try Ehud's brutal murder of Eglon, the fat man king of Moab. Or for tragic family horrors, look no farther than the story of Amnon's rape of Tamar, and his eventual murder at the hands of Absalom—all of them David's own children.

But sexuality? For that, nothing surpasses David's affair with Bathsheba, a woman so drop-dead gorgeous that when David, the man closest to God's own heart, ogles her while bathing, he falls into such a frenzy that eventually he stops at nothing, not even murder, to cover his lousy tracks.

And yet, the whole sordid affair with Bathsheba inspired David to write one of the most beautiful poems in the Bible, Psalm 51. It includes one of the most memorable phrases, a line that has become the centerpiece of many hymns. "Create in me a clean heart, O God," he says in verse 10. Remembering how low David must have felt when finally confronted by the truth, only a heartless person could miss the depth of David's suffering in the urgency of his plea for forgiveness.

But there's another line in Psalm 51 that's really fascinating. You must remember, of course, that in order to cover up the fact that he'd made her pregnant, David deliberately sent her husband, Uriah, to the front of the battle line so that Uriah would come home in a body bag. But in verse 4 of Psalm 51, David says: "Against you, you only, have I sinned." Doesn't that line seems a bit narrow, really? David had sinned against Bathsheba; he'd sinned against Uriah; he'd even sinned, in a way, against his own people. Yet, he says to God, "against you only," as if only God really counts.

What David understands is that our sin is, first of all, war against the King of Peace. Restitution must be undertaken all right; forgiveness must be found. But God is not only our judge in such cases; he's also, significantly, the victim of our treachery.

The passage from Numbers 5 that we've read for today deals with restitution—in other words, making up for the crime. The law God whispers into Moses' ear is very clear: If you steal an ox from your neighbor's flock of cattle, you pay him what that ox is worth—plus a fifth more. That's restitution. You steal, you pay. It's that simple.

Two nights ago I heard a prison chaplain say that one of the most wonderful programs he oversees in the prison where he works is a program designed to bring the criminal and the victim back together in a kind of restitution. That's where he's seen miracles occur, he said.

But parity plus a fifth isn't the last word of this passage. If the victim has no close relative to cash the check, then payment must still be made—to God. Restitution, in that case, belongs to the Lord.

God Almighty is, in his own way, the victim of all of our crimes, all of our sin. We owe *him* too. That's the spirit of this regulation. He's no objective, third-party observer to our sin. When we sin, God Almighty, creator of heaven and earth, is also violated.

With God as our ruler, there's no such thing as a victimless crime.

It is almost unimaginable for us to think that our sin hurts you, Lord, no matter whether what we do is a crime or just an errant thought. Forgive us, Lord, whenever we sin against you. Forgive us always. Amen.

MEDITATION 11

ORDEAL BY HOLY WATER

Read Numbers 5:11-28.

A kid named Moloch got into trouble recently. He was so mad at his sister—she'd stolen his crystals—that he took her whole collection of mouse tails and buried them under a railroad bridge.

His sister, Maribel, found out. She was furious. Maribel told their mother, Luzania, who gives new meaning to the word *bizarre*. Moloch, accused by Maribel of the crime, denied it in front of Luzania.

Luzania had just been reading the book of Numbers. She said she would try her own version of an ancient way of determining truth. Moloch, she said, would have to sleep at the edge of the swamp for four nights—no tent, no screen, no insect repellent. If he returned from the swamp with no mosquito bites, he would be declared innocent and falsely accused.

This strange family lives in northern Minnesota, where mosquitoes are so plentiful they've been known to set up their own slow-pitch tournaments. So when Moloch came back from the swamp, he had to be put in a straitjacket to keep him from itching himself into insanity.

Now I know that's a weird story, but so is the one in today's passage—ordeal by holy water. It makes most scholars roll their eyes.

Let's review it. A man *thinks* his wife is having an affair; he doesn't *know*. So he takes her to the priest, along with a small shopping bag full of barley for the proper jealousy offering.

The priest takes holy water out of a jar, dumps in a little dust from the floor of the temple—special dust—loosens the woman's hair, and puts the barley in her hands. Then he tells her about the trial he's about to create—if she's innocent, she won't get sick. If she gets sick, her husband was right. He makes the woman repeat it, oath-like.

The priest writes all this down, then washes off the paper in the holy water. Then the woman drinks the water. You've got to be really thirsty to like it.

If the woman's thighs get skinny and her stomach bloats (this may well be a way of saying that she becomes unable to have any more

children), then, the priest says, she's guilty of the affair. If not, she isn't. That's easy enough.

If her husband was wrong, it seems to me he ought to have his toes roasted; but in fact, false accusation appears to have been no big deal at all.

Weird. Very, very weird.

The ordeal by holy water is a test whose ability to determine truth rests on the belief that God's own hand will work a miracle to determine innocence or guilt. The trial trusts in God—not in eyewitnesses, clear evidence, obvious motives, or good arguments.

Shouldn't we trust God too? Of course. Shouldn't we bring God into our legal system like the Israelites did? After all, look at what it says right here in the Bible.

Baloney!

This passage is God's word for his wilderness people in the middle of their wanderings. As interesting as the whole story of the exodus is, as important as it is in understanding how God loves his people, the Lord doesn't want us to scrap our court system in favor of trial by holy water or mosquito-infested swamp, just as he doesn't want us, today, to make people with skin rashes clear out of town.

Fascinating stuff—even instructive; but for us, only that.

Thank you, Lord, for your holy Word. Help us to read it and understand how much you love us, how much you care and how much you have always cared for your people. But help us to read it and understand it correctly too. Help us to know you better. Amen.

MEDITATION 12

THE FRUIT OF THE VINE

Read Numbers 6:1-4.

My mother is going to blush when I tell you this story. She might even be disgusted, but that's my problem. I'll tell you anyway.

She's seventy-five years old—I'd better get this right. In her whole life she hasn't had all that many drinks (by *drinks,* I mean the type laced with a touch of liquor). Maybe I'm wrong about the number. Maybe she's slipped in a few since I've been gone—I don't know. I've been out of their house for a long time.

I'm already in trouble. I can feel it. So before you get any ideas, let me say this: my mother's no drinker.

Anyway, several years ago she went to a wedding that must have rivaled that famous one at Cana, the place where party goers blew up when the hosts ran out of wine. The wedding my mother attended offered a reception called an "icebreaker," a time for having a drink so the people who didn't know each other would loosen up and have a good time.

And here comes the embarrassing part. My mother actually *liked* the icebreaker. "We had a drink, and you know," she said, somewhat guiltily and somewhat shocked, "that drink made it easier to get to know all those people around you."

Now you have to understand that my mother is as pious a Christian as I've ever met. She's not likely to tell her preacher what she told me, so to me it was—when she admitted it—quite the odd revelation. Ask her sometime. She'll blush.

But she shouldn't have to. The psalms say that "wine gladdens the heart." A little drink can loosen you up—even the Bible says so. You forget yourself a bit, shelf the shyness. For some people, that's not all bad.

The Bible passage we begin today holds special instructions for those Israelites wishing to be Nazirites (not to be confused with Nazarines—Jesus of Nazareth was a Nazarine). Apparently, some people chose to become Nazirites for a time in their lives as a sign of special devotion to God. Some—among them Samson and Samuel—were Nazirites for life.

The big rule for people who wanted to live in such special devotion was to stay away from booze—they couldn't touch the vines. (Some people thought grape leaves were a real treat—and some people today still eat them.) No wine, no liquor of any type, for as long as one chose to be a Nazirite. Why? The Bible also says, "Wine is a mocker." And it is. No question. A little sip of John Barleycorn may help you to lose yourself, but then again, a few more and you may find yourself unceremoniously in the wedding cake.

But there's more. In almost all of the pagan rituals of the Canaanite tribes, some kind of fermented drink was used to stimulate what those people thought to be communication with the gods. Drunkenness, the pagan prophets claimed, was the state of mind essential to hearing the gods speak.

The God of the Israelites wants no part of such silliness. I want you, wholly and completely, he says—not some drunken lout. Come to me with your senses intact, clearheaded, able to listen.

Let's face it: booze is incredibly dangerous, especially to those who believe they need it to become somebody they're not. Drinking devastates lives—it slays both the users and their families, and often as not, innocent victims.

What God wants from the Nazirites is clearheaded devotion, not half-potted prayers. But he also doesn't want to be confused with any other god or ceremony. Pagan deities aren't any more gods than the drunken sots who worship them. Only the I AM is God. On that point, the God of heaven and earth doesn't want his people bleary-minded. He wants all of us to get that straight.

Lord, help us to come to you with our minds clear, our hearts pure. Forgive us when we find ourselves distracted from your will for us. Make all our days into worship. Amen.

MEDITATION 13

BELL-BOTTOMS AND HAIRBOYS

Read Numbers 6:5-12.

My kids swear they won't wear bell-bottom jeans. Sure. Last week in the mall, I saw a salesclerk wearing a faded pair she could have hauled out of a closet full of clothes from twenty-five years ago. Bell-bottoms are coming in. Beware.

If I were a betting man, I'd bet against my kids' resolution. Bell-bottom jeans came out when I was in high school, back in the olden days, and I remember thinking how those broom-like bottoms, sweeping over leather-sandaled feet, would never be—well—me.

Guess what? I wore them. Likely as not, so will my kids, if those billowy jeans ever become high fashion again.

Bell-bottoms, sandals, long hair, beards, beads, flowers—all that hippie stuff was part of my youth, part of a culture everybody called "counterculture." That meant kids with bell-bottoms, at least at first, thought themselves different from kids with flat-top haircuts, high school letter sweaters, and stovepipe pants—fifties-type preppies.

In the sixties, in the U.S. at least, if you dressed "counterculture" it likely meant that you had certain views on certain issues—for instance, it's likely you opposed the war in Vietnam. At least most bell-bottomed hairboys opposed it.

I remember walking down a street in Saugatuck, Michigan, in the summer of 1968, my hair quite long, and simply meeting, in passing, a guy with similarly long locks. We said hi. I didn't know the guy from Dick Clark. But we both had long hair, and therefore we both simply assumed we shared a whole raft of similar political positions. Long hair made us compatriots. Strange, but true.

The Nazirites were "hairboys" too (remember Samson?). Short-term Nazirites, who wanted to spend only a month or two in serious, methodical devotion to God, are told in today's passage that in addition to avoiding wine, they should let their hair grow. And lest I become sexist, let's make clear that women, too, could be Nazirite "hairgirls."

In a way, the Nazirites were also "counterculture." A Nazirite's long hair was meant to draw attention to a person out of the ordinary. It was a kind of visual indication of her dedication to God. And letting hair grow for religious reasons wasn't unique to the Israelites. Even today, some Islamic people let their hair grow when they make a pilgrimage to Mecca.

Long hair is a lot easier to understand than it is to manage. But what on earth does all of this morbid body stuff in today's passage have to do with being devoted to God?

Again, we've got to go back a long way, to another culture altogether. Unlike today, disease—and death—were thought to be the work of demons. Back then, having cancer would have meant the devil was burrowing into your lymph nodes. No one believes that today; in fact, I know people who claim that their bout with cancer brought them closer to God. But the Israelites believed that any disease was a sign of Satan; they could see Old Scratch in a skin rash.

So in those days, touching a dead body, a diseased body, meant touching a body doused with demons. And that was not only dangerous, it was sinful.

God wants cleanliness from the Nazirites. He demands purity. If Nazirites are to seek him vividly, they need to come to him undefiled. That's the law he plants in Moses' ear.

Though it's not anywhere in the Bible (in fact, it was John Wesley who coined the phrase), for Israel, and especially the Nazirites, cleanliness *is* next to godliness.

So what's the moral of the story? Don't pray with mud on your shoes? Don't be silly. What God wants of us is our very best selves, no matter how long we wear our hair.

Dear Lord, help us give ourselves to your will purely in everything we do. Whether we install roofs or milk cows or type up reports, may all our work praise your name. Amen.

MEDITATION 14

GIFTS

Read Numbers 7:1-5.

In our church, every week somebody gets up front and asks the whole congregation for special concerns to pray about. Some people raise their hands and tell him or her their joys and concerns; then the one who asked, prays. I envy people who can stand up and pray as beautifully as those people do. There's no way I could do that.

I've got a friend who's seventy-four years old, a retired nurse. She spends months every year in places so primitive people go to bed when the sun goes down, not because they turn out the lights but because there are none. Shoot, I couldn't live without the evening news.

Some people I know talk so passionately about how they love the Lord that sometimes I wonder if I even place in the Lord's eyes—you know what I mean? I can't do that. Some people thank him for absolutely everything—sun and rain, robins and grouchy grackles, good times and bad. People like that seem so close to God.

If a farmer gets sick around here, a half dozen of his neighbors will harvest all of that guy's corn and soybeans in just a day or two. They'll take time right out of their own busy harvest schedules to help out. I never do anything as noble as that.

I know a woman who said that once, when her husband was out of work, a wonderful old lady in church sneaked her a check for a hundred dollars. "You just spend it on yourself," the old woman told her. "Everything you have goes to those kids of yours, and you need something yourself once in awhile." My friend claims that gift was the very best present she ever received in her life. I hardly ever think about other people.

One of my former students lives in Somalia and the Sudan, where people live in the most horrible conditions. He works there, helping to bring relief to the starving. In my whole life, I don't think I've ever seen a really hungry child.

I know people who go to the state prison every week—every week—just to visit the prisoners. They do a Bible study for the convicts every Tuesday of the year. I can't believe it. Imagine giving away one whole night of every week for something like that!

Some women—busy women at home and on the job—make meals for other people's families, families with special problems, even though those women have all they can do to keep up with the busyness of their own lives. What I want to know is, where do they find time to do it?

Chapter 7 of the book of Numbers has to rank as one of the most long-winded chapters in the Bible—it's one huge list of the gifts the separate tribes of Israel brought to the tabernacle of the Lord. Every gift is listed; everyone is remembered.

Somewhere—right now maybe—somebody reading this may well be wishing he or she could write meditations like the one you're looking at.

I can't pray out loud very well. I don't think of others as much as I should. I'm not good at talking to people who have suffered real pain. I'm often too busy to do the kinds of little things that mean a lot to other people.

But I write these things.

Everyone—really, *everyone*—has gifts. Some look more glamorous than others. Some haul in more money or fame. Some get much more attention. But everybody does something well.

This long chapter seems to imply that everybody's talents are important to the God who accepts our gifts, every last one of them—simply because he loves the givers.

Help us to know what our gifts are, Lord, and help us to help others know theirs. Make us kind and considerate, and build up the confidence we need to be sure that we are doing your will in our lives. Amen.

MEDITATION 15

QUESTIONS AND ANSWERS

Read Numbers 9:1-14.

There is no good way of explaining what happened other than to say that Rodney Malarky is just plain annoying.

He wears dumb T-shirts his mother buys him, and he's got no arms to speak of—he looks starved, like one of those malnourished children in some desolate place. But it isn't his looks that make him annoying. It's the way he shadows people. He does this clinging thing. He'll follow you like exhaust, even if you don't ask him.

And he's always saying stupid stuff. Like if he sees you in a store and you're about to buy a Coke or something, he'll say, "Hey, about to get yourself a Coke?"

No, stupid, having my lips pierced.

That kind of thing. Annoying.

And he's always talking about his old man. Just the other day, Jeff's talking about doing this all-night catfishing thing sometime, you know—just us guys. Get my tent down by the river, start a nice little fire, roast hot dogs and marshmallows, and all the time you got your lines in waiting for some king catfish. This great all-nighter.

All of a sudden, Rodney—who nobody asked along anyway—says, "My dad caught this lunker bass one time—four pounds." And he stretches his arms open like it's a big deal.

We all look at him, like, who cares, dodo?

So anyway, Tuesday Jeff spots Rodney's bike up on the porch at his cousin's place. The lights are out, except in the basement; so Jeff gets this nasty idea. Steal the dork's bike.

He doesn't break the spokes or jam the gears. He carries it down off the front porch—it's getting dark outside—and takes off, telling me to pick him up at the railroad tracks behind the old shoe factory.

He doesn't throw it down or anything. Just hides it. That factory's been dead for years. Nobody ever goes back there.

Rodney's parents blow a head gasket. Okay, I'll admit it—Malarky's got a decent bike, a Diamond Back. Probably cost a fortune. The next day, Rodney's shaking like a leaf he's so mad or scared or maybe both. He runs around all over, telling people his parents are going to stiff him good for losing it or else stick the culprits in jail.

Jeff's an okay guy. He didn't mean any harm. But this thing got way out of hand. "Don't you dare tell," he says to me. "You know what Malarky's parents are like—Hitler had nothing on them. I'll get hung."

So two nights later I do what I think is the right thing and bring the bike back myself. I wait until dark and drive it up the alley behind Rodney's place and leave it behind the garage. The only way to get out of this alive, I figure.

Sorry. Rodney's uncle, who's putting garbage in the dumpster, sees me, and that night yet, Rodney's parents are on the phone to mine, ready to tear my hide off.

So what do I do?—that's what I want to know. Grabbing his Diamond Back wasn't my idea anyway, not from the start. But I don't want to get Jeff in trouble either. I don't want to squeal. Besides, we didn't mean it mean, if you get my drift.

I've been up in my room here for two nights now, grounded. All month.

Sometimes I wish I could just call up God and find out what's the best thing to do. Like in the Bible, people just say, "Well, God, what do I do?" And he, like, answers them.

I wish it were that easy. I hate being grounded.

It wasn't just Jeff's fault. I could have stopped him.

I don't know what to do. I wish God would tell me.

We get ourselves in pickles, Lord, get ourselves in tough positions where it seems there's no way to turn and nowhere to go. In times like that, Lord, help us to know what's right. Speak to us clearly and lead us not into temptation. In Jesus' name, Amen.

MEDITATION 16

FREEDOM'S BURDEN

Read Numbers 9:15-23.

From the day she turned sixteen, Aletha wanted her own place, her own apartment. She wanted to come and go as she pleased and make her own decisions. That sounded like adulthood to her, doing her own thing.

So when she graduated from high school, she got an assembly-line job making computer monitors and hauled in enough money to finally—happy day!—rent her own place: one bedroom, a little kitchen, and a living room where she put up a bookcase her father told her how to make—bricks from a lumberyard along with a few cheap planks of pressed wood. Her dad picked up a used TV, and Aletha fit her old boom box on its own shelf. She called the bookcase her own entertainment center.

Phone?—sheesh, should she buy or rent one? She drove back home that first Sunday for a meal, and her dad told her he thought it might be smarter to buy. And yes, he had some old silverware in a closet somewhere she could have. For a while at least, he said, she could use the pans they'd used for camping. "They're not that bad," he said.

The apartment came with a stove, a refrigerator, and a bed; but she needed a couch. "I don't know what to buy," she told her father.

So the next Saturday he picked her up, and the two of them hit all the garage sales in the southeast corner of the city. Fortunately, he'd borrowed Fred Baker's truck, so they could haul the stuff home.

"You all set now?" her father said when he let her off.

She told him she thought so.

"I haven't had your car in for months," her father said. "Does it need a tune-up?"

"How do I know?" Aletha said, her eyebrows peaked.

He told her how she had to watch the mileage scribbled on the little tag on the door, how she couldn't afford not to change the oil.

"Where do I bring it?" she said.

"You've got to find a mechanic around here somewhere—"

"I don't know anybody," she told him.

"Look in the phone book," he said.

"Under what?"

"*Mechanics*—I don't know. *Car repair*, maybe, just look."

"Then what?'

"Then call."

"What do I say?"

Her dad rolled his eyes. "Tell him you want your hair done," he told her, trying to be cute. "Tell him you want an oil change, for pete's sake—"

"Me?"

"Trust me, he'll understand."

Being on your own means making millions of decisions you might never have thought about. When the Israelites finally made it out of captivity, they didn't know much about freedom because, as slaves, they'd never made their own decisions.

Today's passage shows how completely dependent the ex-slaves were on God's leading. When the cloud floated, they followed. When it sat still, so did they. They were hardly on their own.

They didn't know much at all about making decisions. They were a people who had to trust in the God who'd delivered them from slavery into the sometimes puzzling world of freedom. Sure they were free—but that didn't mean they didn't need a whole lot of guidance.

And so do we.

Lord, help us when we think we're totally on our own. Often you remind us that we need you—and that we need your people. We like to think of ourselves as free, but we know that without you, we are nothing at all. Thank you for your love. Amen.

MEDITATION 17

ORDER AND CHAOS

Read Numbers 10:11-28.

Everybody knows at least one story just like this.

Mr. Abrams has two beautiful little kids with bright eyes and sparkling personalities. His wife is dear too. She plays the organ in church and runs a preschool out of their split-foyer house in a nice suburb.

Mr. Abrams himself plays a mean trumpet. When he was in college, he was a star, doing solos every time the band did a concert anywhere. He loved music so much that he figured the only way he could keep making it—he didn't think he was good enough to be a pro—was to teach it.

So he took a job at a school near you.

As a trumpet player, he was astounding; as a teacher he bombed.

He had sixty-four kids in band, and the first year he taught he came into a system that had gone through three music teachers in the last five years. The kids were wild, way out of control. Band was a joke to all of them, and Abrams just wasn't the type to kick butt—if you know what I mean. He hated to yell, and what made it worse, the kids knew it. The only human being capable of bringing that crowd into line was Wyatt Earp.

When Abrams was a kid, nobody ever had to stand over him with a club to make him practice. Nobody ever scolded him into playing "Stars and Stripes Forever." But when he got into the classroom where his kids didn't give a hoot about tooting, they just about killed him. He lost sleep, weight, hair, and, toughest of all, self-respect. He even cried in class.

The first year was a disaster—tipped music stands, gum in mouthpieces, four broken drums—just a mess. He sent a constant stream of kids to the principal's office.

The second year wasn't much better. In fact, it was worse. At contract time, the school board told him that he wouldn't be rehired, so he resigned, saving the public humiliation, even though everyone knew he'd been fired.

A few kids were upset, and lots of parents wrung their hands. Everybody felt terrible for this young guy and his young family, since

Mr. Abrams was suddenly out of a job he thought he'd wanted so badly. It was awful.

But the school board had no choice, not really. The fact is, Abrams' music room was absolute chaos, a madhouse, a zoo—insane. For two years parents had complained. The school board had no choice.

I've made this story up, but chances are when you read over it, you're probably thinking of some teacher you know—maybe language arts, math, maybe art or social studies. Such things happen, unfortunately—and quite often.

The fact is, chaos is disaster. As dumb as rules can be sometimes, imagine life without them. Imagine life without police, without courts, without somebody in charge. Ask people from Somalia what it's like, or Rwanda, or Serbia. Chaos is madness. Somebody breaks into your house, but there's no police to call. What do you do? Pick up a gun.

Trust no one. Build a fort and keep that gun drawn to keep intruders away, keep everybody away. Spend every hour afraid.

Murder goes unpunished. Men rape at will. The most deadly guns win. You stay off the streets because vicious gangs of toughs roam like mad dogs.

Everything we've read so far in the book of Numbers has to do with order, and it's not hard to see why. This swarm of Israelites, about to begin tramping through the wilderness with their backpacks and their oxen, are a disaster waiting to happen if there's no order, no laws, no authority.

Everything God tells Moses is meant to shape this swarm into something strong enough to take the ordeal ahead of them. Now it's time to get going.

Lord, be with those people who live in lands where there is no order. Be with those who suffer at the hands of lawlessness and chaos. Help us to act whenever and however we can as a shining light and helping hand to those who see no hope. Amen.

MEDITATION 18

HOBAB THE MIDIANITE AND THE QUESTION OF FAITH

Read Numbers 10:29-35.

Read over today's passage and you might think that thousands of years ago already some rotten scoundrel tried to scuttle our faith in the Bible as God's Word by sneaking in this puzzling little tale of Hobab.

Who is this Hobab anyway? Read verse 29 again. Is he Moses' brother-in-law or his father-in-law? In my study Bible, a footnote claims Hobab was his brother-in-law. A lot of scholars aren't even sure. What we know is this: he's a Midianite, like Moses' first wife, Zipporah. And we know he knows his way around the wilderness.

In fact, that's what Moses likes about the guy. "We're about to go to the promised land, Hobab," Moses tells him. "Don't desert us now."

Moses has faith—let's not miss that point. He doesn't think the Lord God of Israel has been joshing his people about their future in this rich dreamland he's promised them.

But Hobab, who knows his way around, says he's going home.

"Hold on," Moses says. "You know every watering hole between here and Asia Minor." Then he says something really odd: "You can be our eyes."

Whoa! Unless your memory is worse than mine, only a few dozen verses back we discovered how this holy cloud now sits over the tabernacle in the heart of the encampment. The Israelites moved when it did, and they kept their tent stakes in the earth when that cloud sat still. The Israelites already had their guide, didn't they? Moses knows that. Why on earth does he think he needs Hobab to point out the best camping spots when the Lord God Almighty already gave them the holy cloud—one that's on fire too!

All of a sudden here's Hobab, like the guy who dropped out of the sky and into the ring of the world championship boxing match in Las Vegas. This is some kind of joke.

But there's more mystery. "So they set out from the mountain"—that's the way the next verse begins. What about Hobab, the Daniel Boone of the Midianites? Did he come or go? What happened here?

It's really not clear at all. One strange little episode.

Did Moses' asking Hobab to stay around mean Moses lacked faith in the holy cloud? Maybe Moses is just as slick as some of the Israelites think he is. Lots of people think he has mega-faith, but really he's an operator, pulling some strings behind the curtain.

I doubt it. The rest of the chapter shows clearly how the cloud led the Israelites; even quotes the holy songs Moses chanted. So don't accuse Moses of lack of faith—at least not yet.

Then what's the deal here? What does this passage mean?

We'd all love E-mail answers, on-line from God, the kind Moses seemed to get every afternoon. Anyone who believes in God would love to actually hear his voice. It booms, I bet: "Andrea, go to Mexico." Wouldn't that be great—even if it were only a whisper?

Even though I've never received that kind of God-mail, I know I've been spoken to—my conscience screams sometimes, as a matter of fact. Occasionally, God puts suffering in front of me to make me react. He brings me into rooms full of pain and tells me to come closer to things I'd rather not see. God communicates to all of us through the Bible, of course, as well as in the things "of this world."

Moses wants the best for his people. He's working hard at it, not only by keeping himself on-line with God's E-mail, but also by his sense of what's good business. Keeping Hobab around is just plain good sense because he's too full of wilderness savvy to let go.

"Stay around," Moses says. "We need you." That's not lack of faith, I guess. It's just common sense.

There are times, Lord, when we become so filled with your goodness that we can almost forget we're in your world. Thank you for our moments of spirit-filled enthusiasm, but help us to remember you want our obedience in what we do from day to day. Amen.

MEDITATION 19

THE WHINERS

Read Numbers 11:1-3.

When the Shelbys go on vacation, Dad has to have everything just so—if you know what I mean. They always leave just before dawn, but they pack the car already the night before. And it's always done the exact same way: the kids haul the stuff out to the car, plop it down on the driveway, and leave it there.

Only Dad packs. Nobody else. To him, packing is a science. The idea is to take the suitcases, the sleeping bags, the toiletries, the kitchen stuff, the tent, the stakes and the poles—take the whole mess and make it fit together into something that resembles one of those little Chinese wooden puzzles.

Of course, Mom's the same way about packing bags—socks in shoes, shoes in bags, bags in suitcases—like the toy rooster you take apart only to find a little banty hen, then another, and then another.

Morning comes. Dad's alarm goes off, he gets up, puts on coffee, makes sure everything's in good shape, while Mom goes through the bathroom one more time—toothpaste? check; hair spray? check; fingernail clipper, check; Band-Aids—who forgot the Band-Aids?

Aaron's the oldest. He wakes up immediately, puts on the clothes he'd laid out the night before, then sits waiting at the kitchen table as if this is all taking far too long. Mom and Dad wake up the other kids, who seem startled but bounce out of bed as if they'd been already dreaming of leaving. They lug their pillows downstairs, jump in the back seat, and immediately proceed to giggle. It's always the same.

Dad backs out of the driveway, pauses with car's rear end nudging into the street, then turns to Mom to make sure they've got everything. She nods. They leave. The car is in perfect silence, the glow of dawn over their shoulders as they drive west.

Aaron pushes Brady's foot off his lap. Brady pretends to be asleep and floats his foot back on his brother's side. Aaron pushes it again. Brady moans angrily.

Dad's worried. The car's transmission surges between gears, almost jerks, clumsily. Tiny raindrops speckle the windshield. He wonders about the hatchet. He told Aaron to pack it, but he didn't see it.

Brady's foot, accidentally on purpose, kicks Aaron, even though Brady is sleeping, supposedly. "Cut it out," Aaron says.

Mom looks back. The rain on the windshield gets stronger. As they leave town, they get behind a cattle truck that moves so slowly they could as well have been on the Oregon Trail. Dad can't pass.

"Ouch," Brady yells. He whines, pretends to be hurt. You can hear it's pretend. Mom turns around, doesn't speak. "He hurt me," Brady says. "Tell Aaron not to."

"Tell him to get his feet off me," Aaron snarls.

"I didn't—"

And just like that Dad explodes. Boom! "Here we are eight miles away from home," he says, "and all you can do is complain."

Sound familiar? Happens to the best of us. Happens to families so strong you'd think they lift weights together. Happens to all of us.

It happened even to the Israelites. Whiners. The sun isn't even up yet, and there are things to complain about—irritations, aggravations.

My word, folks, this is going to be a long, long trip.

When we hear the complaints of the Israelites, Lord,
it's easy to think they're ungrateful. But so are we.
Forgive us for whining. Fill us with your Spirit.
Amen.

MEDITATION 20

BURN OUT, BURN-OUT, OR BURNOUT

Read Numbers 11:4-15.

According to my *Oxford American Dictionary*, *burnout* is one word. I don't know who polices the English language, but whoever does the dirty work determined that *burn* and *out*, after living in common-law union so long together, deserved to get themselves hitched. So it's been done. What was two words has become one—*burn out* is officially *burnout.*

These things happen over time, and not often understandably. For instance, *bedroom* has been one word forever almost; *living room,* even though almost every house has one of those too, is still two words. I don't know why.

After two words date long enough, somebody hitches them up with a hyphen—as in *burn-out.* Call that an engagement, maybe. But then, when it's clear that those two words intend to stay together for a long, long time, they're joined in holy matrimony no linguist would dare tear asunder. That's the story on *burnout.* They've now formed a happy union. Go ahead, start tinkling your drinking glass.

And it's right they should be happy. Burnout, in today's world, is as common as a runny nose. When I was a kid, I remember futurists saying that in the years ahead, people would work less and less and less, and devote much more time to "leisure activities." Guess what? "Leisure activities" went the way of the "leisure suit."

Research now indicates that men and women in North America are working more and more and more hours every year. The pressure's on to accumulate moolah; real yuppies know the only way to afford a castle in the 'burbs is with big bucks.

Work your head off—and your tail—and what happens? Burnout. Teachers, social workers, CEO's, accountants burn out—so do preachers, preschool workers, pediatricians. Even parents. Even writers. Like I said, common as a runny nose. It's like a plague.

Want to know what burnout sounds like? Listen to this: "Why have you brought this trouble on your servant? What have I done to displease you that you put the burden of all these people on me? Did I conceive all these people? Did I give them birth? Why do you tell me to carry them in my arms, as a nurse carries an infant, to the land you promised on oath to their forefathers? Where can I get meat for all these people?"

That's what burnout sounds like. Notice the rhetorical questions piled one atop the other—six of them, in fact, none of them really intended to be answered as much as to vent deep frustration. Notice the sarcasm—"Am I their mother or something?" Notice the weariness—"Am I supposed to carry them all on my back?" Notice the personal pronouns. Moses could well have said, "I've had it." Moses is beat, burned out.

But we shouldn't blame him; after all, it wasn't Moses who decided manna every day was dreadfully boring, a lousy substitute for corn-fed marbled sirloin. Moses wouldn't be burned out if it weren't for the hair-trigger whining done by the Israelites.

What he needs is to take a nice long Canadian vacation, sit on an empty lake somewhere, all by himself, and catch walleyes. He's burned out (that's still two words, by the way), and you can tell it all the way from here—thousands of years later.

But there will be no walleye morning for Moses, no quiet lake, no loon medley in the quiet of the evening. For Moses life is a wilderness.

How did we say it yesterday?—"My word, folks, this is going to be a long, long trip."

Thank you for being our shelter in the time of storm, Lord, and thank you also for being our shelter in the time when we create our own storms. Give us peace and strength and confidence in our work. Amen.

MEDITATION 21

TALKING TRASH

Read Numbers 11:16-23.

On the most serious basketball courts in the nation, the courts on playgrounds in this country's inner cities, I'm told that "talking trash" is as much a part of the game as a pull-up jump shot off a fast break. "Talking trash" probably originates in the inner city; it refers to two players jostling each other with words, squaring off as if they'll beat each other silly.

"I get the ball next time, man, and I'll blow around you like you're standing still," Sam says to Wally, throwing an elbow.

"Fat chance," Wally says, using more language I won't quote.

It's winning by intimidation, and good coaches try to keep their kids from doing it. It's unsportsmanlike. It's trashy, even ugly.

When I was a kid, it was unsportsmanlike to annoy the other team's free-throw shooter. I remember cheerleaders trying to shush an unruly crowd because distracting an opponent like that seemed, well, uncivil.

Guess what? That era is long gone. Ball players all over the place are now "talking trash," trying to mess with the quality of the opponent's game by intimidation. Charles Barkley does it, Michael Jordan did it—shoot, everyone does it.

When I hear the Lord talk to Moses in today's passage, I can't help it—I hear God "talking trash." I don't mean to be silly or sacrilegious, and if it's a sin to think that, then I repent here and now. But that's what I hear. Listen.

The Lord sees what is vividly clear: Moses is burned out. So before God deals with the manna-murmurers, he knows he's got to take care of his appointed leader. He tells Moses he's going to take the weight off his back by spreading the work around a little; he asks Moses to pick out seventy leaders. He says he'll ordain them for service that will bring a little rest and relaxation to poor old Moses.

Then he starts in on his people. Now we might look back for just a minute at this whole manna-complaint bellyache. Verse 4 of this chapter claims that the moaning and groaning started with "the rabble," with the weakest, not the strongest.

But just like in the golden calf story, everybody catches the feeling eventually: "Moses heard the people of *every* family wailing," verse 10 says, "each at the entrance to his tent." What prompts Moses' frustration is that eventually everybody's doing it.

"Yes," says God, "tell the people I've heard them say that they had it better in Egypt. I've heard their groaning, and I'm going to answer their bellyaching." Here comes God, talking trash. "You won't eat meat for just one day, or two days, or five, ten or twenty days, but for a whole month [I'm quoting now—this is straight out of the Bible]—until it comes out of your nostrils and you loathe it."

Your image of the Lord God of the universe may be soft and loving and sweet, gentle as Charmin tissue. But here's a picture of an angry, frightfully intimidating, trash-talking God. Here's an image of God that's right in your face. "Because you have rejected the LORD, *who is among you* [who's right here in your camp, God says], I'll give you quail until it erupts from your nose."

Moses, the skeptic, says, "Get serious, Lord. We've got six hundred thousand people in this swarm."

And God says, "You'll see."

Moses does. And so do the whiners.

You are a righteous God, Lord, and you know our most secret lives. Cleanse us from our sin and make us white as snow. Keep us in your love. Amen.

MEDITATION 22

A LESSON IN LEADERSHIP

Read Numbers 11:26-30.

The passage for today is not "the love scene," "the fight to the finish," or "the car chase." It's no nail-biter, but it's a wonderful little scene.

Moses, who not very long ago seemed one little complaint shy of a nervous breakdown, is told to pick out seventy men for a kind of swarm council, a few good men to carry the burden of leadership. He's told to bring them to the tabernacle tent, where God blessed them with his Spirit. "And they prophesied," the Bible says, which means they gave some obvious evidence of being filled with God's Spirit.

Now Eldad and Medad, who were among those chosen by Moses, didn't show up for the swearing-in. The Bible doesn't say why, but their being no-shows doesn't appear to have made any difference in the long run. Even though they weren't there for the ceremony, they prophesied too, just like the others.

Joshua, son of Nun, and no minor character in this epic himself, is miffed about the two tardys. He hustles back to Moses with the news. "My lord," he says, still puffing from the long sprint, "you have to stop those guys."

Now Joshua means well. Eldad and Medad, after all, didn't show up for the ceremony. They weren't there at the tabernacle, and to Joshua they seem like imposters, maybe even sleazy TV evangelists. If Eldad and Medad started acting like big shots, started drawing a crowd at the camp, Joshua likely figured any Tom, Dick, or Harry could do the same thing. And then what would happen? It's chaos, Moses. Do something.

Then comes a great line, a line that takes some thought. Moses turns to Joshua and says, "Are you jealous for my sake?"

Now there are two ways of understanding what Moses means here, and really, both of them make sense. The first way cuts a bit: Moses might simply mean "what business is this of yours?" He might have been telling Joshua to mind his own business and get back to the Department of Sanitation or whatever job he'd lined up for the kid.

But I like the way John Calvin looks at this line. When Moses says, "Are you jealous for my sake?" Calvin thinks the emphasis should be put on the word *jealous*, not on *my*. What Calvin thinks Moses is saying is this: It's not *me* or my power that's in question here, Junior—this show belongs to the Lord. Jealousy is not only dumb, it's plain wrong.

I like to think of this line as a lesson in leadership. Moses' response is meant to show the intern Joshua that in God's army there's no room for jealousy; all the power and all the glory belong to the Commander-in-Chief. I like to think of Moses saying it in a soft voice—"Are you jealous for my sake?"—with a kind of wry smile, a bit of understatement that echoes in Joshua's conscience and his soul.

By the way, how about a round of applause for Moses, who just a few verses ago was at his wit's end, so sick of Israel's bellyaching that he was snarling at God? Here, one of his own boys, with the best of intentions, says something Moses sees is plain wrong—"We've got men prophesying in the name of God, and they don't have a license."

Moses says, "Hey, slow down. Don't you wish everybody was filled with God's Spirit?" Really, it's a lesson in leadership. "Don't take this personally, Joshua," Moses says, "because I'm not. I'm overjoyed."

If you want to lead, Moses could have told Israel's future leader, don't forget that in God's army, *leading* means *serving* the King.

I like to think Joshua rather quietly backed out of the room, nodding the whole time.

Forgive our pride, Lord. It's so easy for us to think
we've got the whole truth, and when we do, it's not
hard for us to believe that nobody else does. Our
great joy is in knowing that we belong to you.
Help us not to use your love to play favorites.
In Jesus' name, help us to love. Amen.

MEDITATION 23

GLUTTONY

Read Numbers 11:31-35.

When I was a boy growing up on the shores of Lake Michigan, we never did much fishing—in fact, we never went fishing at all. With good reason—there were no fish. Lampreys, a blood-sucking disaster on game fish, had cleaned out the entire pond.

Maybe twenty years ago, the Department of Natural Resources cleaned out the lamprey population and planted thousands of fingerling trout and salmon. In a few years, *everybody* went fishing in the big lake, and Lake Michigan, along with the other Great Lakes, took its place among the hottest fishing spots in North America. I know a man in Minneapolis, Minnesota, who had a boat completely outfitted with Great Lakes fishing gear, even though he got out on Lake Michigan only a couple times per summer. Tremendous fishing. B-I-G Fish. This big. No joke.

It's cooled down a bit now. Some of the fishing boats that once hauled tourist-fishermen out into the lake have abandoned the harbors. There's still good fishing out there—trout and salmon—but some of the joy is gone because today the fish are sick, unhealthy.

Ten years ago, I used to catch big, fat trout simply by wading into the surf and casting. It was great fun, but even then there were warnings that little kids and nursing mothers shouldn't be eating the bellies of those fish, because that part was usually full of poison. It's too bad.

Out here in Iowa, everybody knows you've got to bake your chops really well done because if you don't, you risk *trichinosis,* a disease caused by eating undercooked pork.

Not so long ago in the state of Washington, several people died from eating the infected meat of hamburgers served up by a Jack-in-the-Box restaurant. Food poisoning isn't all that rare.

You know what else? At least twice a year whole flocks of quail still regularly migrate between Africa and Syria. Bird-watchers who have noticed the phenomenon claim that people can catch them by the dozen at certain times and places, specifically where the birds settle

down, pooped by all their flying. They're remarkably easy to grab, people say, even without nets.

Now let's put two and two together here. The Israelites just happened to be in the quails' flight plan. A huge mob of those birds got tuckered out—like they still do—at just the spot where the Israelite thousands were encamped. Maybe they had a germ or something, like the Lake Michigan game fish, maybe some form of salmonella, some kind of pathogenic bacterium—doesn't that sound scientific?

Anyway, the Israelites let the meat dry out in the sun—not exactly the most healthy idea. Then they gorged themselves, the gluttons, ate themselves sick.

We're not told how many died after eating the quail, but we know that enough did that those who survived named that spot in the wilderness after the mass poisoning. What happened is too bad; but those people were foolish—they shouldn't have eaten all that bad meat. Talk about stupid.

The whole story is quite explainable really. The Bible says it was an act of God, but if you look at it scientifically, it's perfectly understandable. To say that God caused this to happen is a little medieval, don't you think?—almost superstitious? There's a perfectly good scientific explanation for the whole works. God? Bah, humbug.

Sure. Believe that and I've got a bridge I'd like to sell you.

Our human minds are often too skeptical to believe in miracles, Lord, and yet we know that you have power to calm roaring seas, roaring lions, and even roaring human beings. You can do anything, Lord. Help us to see your awesome, miraculous works. Amen.

MEDITATION 24

AMBITION

Read Numbers 12:1-3.

When Daedalus, the master inventor of Greek mythology, fell out of favor with his king, he and his son Icarus were banished to a tower on an island from which there was no obvious means of escape. Daedalus came up with a brilliant idea—why not just fly away? The great inventor created wings of wax and feathers, fitted them on himself and his son, and caught the updrafts. In this way they were able to leave their island prison behind.

But Icarus was so thrilled by his ability to fly that he forgot his father's specific warnings and flew too close to the sun, which melted the wax, destroying the wings and sending him plunging to his death in the sea below.

Lots of people know that story. However, there's another story about Daedalus that most people don't remember.

After his son's death, Daedalus returned to Sicily, where he built a great temple to Apollo and hung up his wings as a kind of tribute to his god. Then he became a teacher.

Unfortunately, this brilliant man Daedalus, who could make most anything with his hands, couldn't stomach rivals. One of his students, Perdix, a son of his sister, mind you, was absolutely brilliant. He created the first saw out of notched iron—copying the pattern he saw in the spine of a fish. Later, Perdix put two pieces of iron together with a rivet and made a pair of compasses—those things you draw circles with. Bright, bright boy with a great future.

When Daedalus, who'd already lost his son, saw how bright this nephew of his was, he chewed himself up inside. He couldn't stand the fact that Perdix might be even more brilliant than he was; so Daedalus, who'd seen his own son die while flying too high, acted.

One day, as they were standing on the top of a high tower, Daedalus pushed Perdix over the edge. Fortunately (all of this is Greek mythology), Minerva, a god who liked crafty people—saw it all and saved Perdix by turning him into a partridge. End of story.

What this character Daedalus shares with Aaron and Miriam from our story is a species of jealousy rooted in ambition. All three had gifts—Daedalus, the great inventor; Aaron, the high priest; and Miriam, his sister, the only woman granted the title of prophetess (Ex. 15:20). (Besides, Aaron and Miriam had had front row seats for every last miracle at Pharaoh's court.)

But then they begin to question Moses' leadership. The first thing they do is claim their own strength: "Hasn't the Lord also spoken through us?" they tell each other, thumbs poking from their suspenders.

The answer is yes. They've been blessed, but what they forgot is that their strength isn't something they've built with their own hands—it's God-given. They think they're hot stuff. "Hey, we can prophesy too—we're big-time."

"The sufficiency of my merit," said Augustine, "is to know that my merit is not sufficient." There's a line that turns right back on itself, and it's not really that difficult to understand. "I'm strong," Augustine could have said, "but only because I know I'm weak enough to know the Lord is my strength."

Aaron and Miriam apparently didn't know either the weakness of their strength or the strength of their weakness.

They learned, though. Just read on. But let me warn you—it's another very sad story.

All our strength in all of our tomorrows comes
from your hand, Lord. Help us to be strong
through all of our lives, but never let us forget that
our strength comes from belonging to your family.
In Jesus' name, Amen.

MEDITATION 25

THE REAL ISSUE

Read Numbers 12:1-3.

There are a couple of loose ends in this story, especially at the beginning. The chapter begins with Aaron and Miriam discussing the fact that Moses, their brother, and the God-appointed leader of his people, had married a Cushite.

Now I don't know what kind of ethnic background you come from, but if you want to understand this grumbling, all you need to do is substitute the name of some ethnic or racial group other than your own, and you've got the nature of Miriam's snide remarks.

That's one issue—Moses married a Cushite, an outsider—not one of us, one of his people.

But then there's this matter of prophecy, the great equalizer. Once Aaron and Miriam have shaken their heads for a while about Moses' "outsider" wife—and what his marriage to her implies about him—they start on the whole business of their being equal to Moses. After all, they prophesy too. "Who said *he* was the only honcho around here?" they whine.

The way the two issues connect is interesting, at least to me. Because the reason they dare to bring up the second issue—the business of power and leadership—is really the first issue: that he married someone who is—well, you know—not "one of us."

Here's a story whose facts I know only from one side, but which I wholeheartedly believe is true. More than a few years ago now, some Laotian people moved to a community and got factory jobs on an assembly line where working quickly was more important than speaking English.

These people were dirt poor, of course, and very, very hard workers. They worked so hard, in fact, that some of the other workers, who didn't sweat as much as they did, began to resent them.

See, what happens sometimes in factories is that people get in a certain kind of rhythm. The whole assembly line slows down at, say 4:00—even though everybody quits at 4:30. It's a kind of teamwork thing, and it happens a lot. I know. I used to work in a factory.

But the Laotians didn't know the unwritten rules. They didn't play the game. They kept right on working, right up until quitting time. They pushed out units like they were going out of style, and the other workers, the ones who'd been there for years, got royally ticked.

Finally, one of the old workers, the white workers, told the boss that she was missing some money from her locker, that she saw one of "those people" hanging around there, and that none of the other workers really trusted "them."

One of "them" was fired.

It doesn't take a prophet to know what was going on there. The problem the old workers had with the new Laotians wasn't thievery, it was industry. What ticked them off was that the Laotians were working harder than they were "supposed to," harder than the unwritten agreement all the workers had. The accusation, in other words, had little or nothing to do with the real gripe.

So it is with Miriam and Aaron. What ticks them off, they say, is the fact that their big-time brother married "one of them." That's unbecoming in a man of his position, they think.

But that's baloney. The real problem here is Miriam and Aaron's ambition. That's the bottom line. There's only one issue here—and that issue is power. Moses has it, they're thinking, and, doggone it, we want it.

Sometimes we use other people—especially their differences from ourselves—as a reason for disliking them or distrusting them, when actually we're thinking only about ourselves. Help us to love as you loved us, totally and completely. Amen.

MEDITATION 26

THE PECKING ORDER

Read Numbers 12:4-8; Hebrews 3:1-6.

Among chickens, I'm told, there's no question about who rules the roost. First, of course, is the lordly rooster, king and lord of the barnyard. He's even been known to chase humans off the lot.

After the biggest rooster comes the second best—maybe two or three other males, depending on how big of a roost a farmer keeps. And then the hens. But even among the egg-layers there's a kind of pecking order, a structure of authority kept in place by the power of the beak. "Stay out of my realm, cluck, or you're sawdust."

Sometimes people use the phrase "pecking order" to indicate the line of command in a business, a government, or even a classroom. In fact, like it or not, wherever two or three gather, there's likely some kind of pecking order. Either by strength or money or athletic ability or good looks, some will keep the others in their place.

God probably wouldn't like me saying that in today's passage he reestablishes a pecking order. Moses never lorded it over others; never kept himself on top by putting down other people. In fact, Moses was the humblest soul on earth (v. 3).

But God tells Miriam and Aaron—and Moses too—that there is a line of importance here. He tells Moses' two sibling rebels that even though they've been appointed priestess and high priest, they shouldn't think of themselves as being the top of the pecking order.

With Moses, the Lord says, when he gathers the three of them at the door of the tabernacle, I speak face to face. With other prophets, he tells them, I reveal myself in dreams, in little visions, which, like riddles (v. 8) need to be figured out. But with Moses, not so.

Imagine Moses' tremendous blessing: he gets to see "the form of the Lord." Only Moses gets God-mail.

The Lord points out the difference as a way of taking the wind out of the arguments of Miriam and Aaron. The fact is, God says, Moses knows a whole lot more than you do. If you don't believe that, you're dead wrong.

On one level are the people of Israel; on another the prophets—the seventy appointed in the last chapter and Aaron and Miriam; and finally, at the top, the Lord's most trusted leader, Moses, the one who actually sees God's form.

(Moses actually *sees* God's form!)

But there's more. In the passage from Hebrews, Paul says that although Moses was faithful, he was faithful only "as a servant." Which is not to say bad things about our man Moses. What Paul means is that in the ultimate human flow chart, even Moses, who sees God's form, is not the chief executive officer.

The incredible thing about Jesus Christ is not so much that he is Lord, or that he is God's servant and ours, but that—and this is what's really incredible—he is *both*, the God/man who was Lord/servant. While he "served" his Father by coming into this world, and "served" us by dying for our sins, he was, through it all, still God Almighty, Creator of heaven and earth.

What's more, that he is Lord should make all the Aarons and Miriams of this world—and that includes you and me—know their place. We are what we are because he has made us strong.

He's king of the barnyard, king of the state house, king of the classroom, king of the backyard, and king of every last corner of our lives.

It's that simple and that stupendous.

Prayer: When we think of your power, Lord, we stand in awe. The same God who watched over the Israelites years and years ago now cares for us. That's enough to take our breath away, Lord. Thank you for loving us, even when we, like the Israelites, don't always deserve it. Amen.

MEDITATION 27

MIRIAM'S LEPROSY

Read Numbers 12:9-10.

1992 was, according to the United Nations, "The Year of the Woman." I'm not sure exactly what that means—proclamations of that type are also heralded for soybeans and soda pop. It's safe to assume though, that the intent was to focus attention on the role of women in the world.

Historians and sociologists claim that, since World War II, the way women see themselves has brought really radical changes in the way all of us "do" life from day to day. What women dream of, what they do, where they work, and how they live their lives is completely different today, at least in North America, than it was fifty years ago.

With the exception of the ostriches among us, those changes have made all of us think differently. Now I'm conscious of including women writers when I choose text for my literature class. Some old Adam and Eve jokes simply are not at all funny—"Anybody know why Adam was created first? So he'd get a chance to say something." (I actually heard a guy tell that one at a church program.)

In addition, some passages of Scripture make me feel uneasy. Today's, for instance. Only Miriam seems to suffer punishment for the rebellion she and her brother undertook together. God punishes her with some kind of horribly disgusting skin disease that looks and acts like leprosy. Leprosy means, of course, banishment—remember all the rules at the beginning of the book of Numbers?

Apparently it's an awful disease. When Aaron pleads with Moses to show some pity for his sister, he compares Miriam's look to that of a stillborn infant, its flesh half eaten away. (I'm sorry, but that's exactly how Aaron describes it.)

But *only* Miriam catches it. Not her big brother, Aaron. Why? I don't know how to explain it myself, but I can tell you what some have argued in the past:

- *Because Miriam started it.* Some people think that the whole evil idea started with her—just as some people think that if it hadn't been for Eve, we'd all still be camped in Eden. But read the passage over—there's no reason to believe that Aaron himself might not have cooked up the plot.

- *Aaron didn't get punished because he was the head of God's own church corps.* It wouldn't look good to have such a prominent authority figure disfigured. That's what John Calvin says. Keep in mind, though, that Calvin was an authority figure of some renown himself.
- *Because Miriam's a woman.* I don't know if that's true, but neither do I know it's false.

What I do know is that the punishment is somewhat fitting. After all, Miriam's sin, like Aaron's, was thinking too much of herself. Her horrible disease would certainly prevent that.

And we know it has an effect on Aaron. Immediately he pleads with Moses on her behalf by confessing their mutual sin. The punishment works on both of them.

But why only Miriam? I don't think anyone knows that answer, and I don't think anyone ever will.

It seems, especially after the Year of the Woman, patently unfair. I hate to throw in the towel so easily, but I know this for sure—I'm not God, and neither was Aaron, and neither was Miriam.

But at least we can say this: by the end of this ugly little story of rebellion, both of them obviously knew that too.

Help us to rely on your love and your power even when we don't always understand why things happen the way they do, Lord. Help us to know that your ways are not ours and that you have your plan for our lives. Amen.

MEDITATION 28

MISSION STATEMENT

Read Numbers 13:13-20.

I happen to be one of those people who believe that if Adam and Eve hadn't chomped into the wrong apple there would be no committees. Maybe you disagree. Some people actually like committee work. Of course, some people eat scorpions. As they say, it takes all kinds.

As for me, I'd choose a root canal before a committee meeting, especially when the committee is composed of people like me—college teachers. You see, one of the most obvious characteristics of a college teacher is the ability to speak well. Because college teachers talk a lot, they get good at it—which is not to say they say much. Unfortunately, college teachers' ability to talk makes for endless meetings.

In addition to that, college teachers often suffer from another problem: they begin to believe their own ideas. After semesters of telling others what to think, they start to believe that what they think is fundamental to the life, health, and peace of the whole human race. After all, they've thought it all through.

Form a committee of college profs, give them a sticky mandate—say, developing four general courses that every college student must take—and then shut the door. A cure for the common cold will be developed before they finish their work.

In spite of all that, committees are essential. If a college or a business wants to function smoothly, people have to participate in the decision-making. Every year I serve on a committee or two in the college where I teach. Sometimes what we do is complete baloney; sometimes it's important.

Committees need something called a "mission statement" so that they know what it is they're doing. Now that may sound really ridiculous, but it's true. Unless the committee knows its own job—its *mandate*—it could wander all over the block (especially if that committee is made up of professors).

Today, wherever two or three are gathered, it seems, there is a mission statement. Colleges have them, of course; so do most schools, even elementary schools. Businesses have them too. And most churches have developed mission statements in the last ten years or so because—so people say—we've got to know what we're doing.

God himself creates a committee of Israelites for the important work of reconnaissance. Take a man from every tribe, he says, and send them up ahead to explore the land I've promised you.

Moses follows the Lord's orders, calls the scouts together, and gives them their mandate, their forty-day mission statement: "See what the land is like and whether the people who live there are strong or weak, few or many. What kind of land do they live in? Is it good or bad? What kinds of towns do they live in? Are they unwalled or fortified? How is the soil? . . ." That's their mandate.

This select committee of leaders are more than just good talkers. In a way, they're real James Bond types. Imagine them under the cover of darkness, peeking out from behind trees, sneaking into strange villages, making themselves inconspicuous. A few good men. They even bring back humongous grapes for a memorable show-and-tell.

It must have been a scary assignment. This A-team would have had plenty of adventures. As we'll see, these stealthy patriots did what they were asked to do, and, unfortunately, more besides.

In a phrase—they forgot their mandate. You'll see. Read on.

Our mandate is clear and simple, Lord. You've told us to love you above all and our neighbors as ourselves. Put your Spirit in us so that we may joyfully carry out the work you've assigned us. In Jesus' name, help us to be your servants. Amen.

MEDITATION 29

"JUST THE FACTS, MA'AM"

Read Numbers 13:26-31.

Maybe you've seen the old TV show *Dragnet*. The star was a poker-faced police sergeant named Joe Friday. Even if you've never seen the show—it started almost forty years ago—you probably recognize the opening notes of its theme music—"dum-de-dum-dum; dum-de-dum-dum." Those four notes have probably become as famous as any four notes ever written.

Joe Friday was so deadpan, he seemed like a machine. He'd go to the scene of a crime and begin questioning whatever witness he could locate. Some hysterical onlooker would spill out the details in an explosion of frantic emotions, and Friday would stop her on a dime. "Just the facts, ma'am," he'd say. That phrase became as memorable as "dum-de-dum-dum."

Reading the scouts' report in today's passage, you might wonder whether Moses directed the boys who did the scouting with the same phrase—"Okay, just the facts, boys."

Because what the scouts say, at least at first, is nothing more than facts. "You were right, the land does flow with milk and honey. Check out these grapes. Their cities have huge walls, and the people who live there make the Chicago Bears look like munchkins. What's more, there are tons of them: Amalekites, Hittites, Jebusites, Amorites—"

Just the facts—that's what they seem to give Moses. Just the facts.

But the next verse implies that these facts had an immediate effect on the people listening. "Then Caleb silenced the people"—that's how the verse starts. Just hearing "the facts" seems to have pushed the people into drawing some very definite, fearful conclusions about this so-called "promised land."

Caleb tries to muzzle the murmuring. "We should go right up there and take the whole region," he says, "because we can do it."

Then, just like that, ten of the scouts, who have been chosen from the best men of Israel, throw in the towel and side with the scared. "We can't attack those people. They're stronger than we are," they scream.

The unbelievers fan out among the people, and the fear they preach grows into a wildfire.

If Sergeant Friday had been there, he'd have slammed his fist down on the table and said "just the facts, boys." Moses may even have tried. But a mob's a mob.

What the Lord God Almighty had sent the scouts out to do—what he'd given them as their mission statement—was to check out the land he'd promised them. Just check it out. "Just the facts."

But ten of the scouts turn out to be spin doctors. They want to control the way the people understand "the facts." Once they've given their report, their own fear comes out in spades. And that fear is obvious to the mob of Israelites listening: "We can't do it—no way. Those men have got huge shoulders. We can't."

Can't. That's the big word. "It *can't* be done."

Ten of the scouts forgot their mandate—"just the facts." They drew conclusions based on their sighting of enemies built like all-pro linebackers. But God hadn't asked them to draw conclusions—it wasn't part of their mandate.

"We *can't,*" they say. And just like that, a forty-day mission became a forty-year campout. And just like that, God Almighty, their glorious deliverer, once again boils in anger. "That's enough," he says.

And that's a fact.

Forgive our unbelief, Lord. Help us to understand how your love and power equip us to meet anything and everything we'll ever meet in this world. Help us to believe in you, even when we aren't so sure about ourselves. Amen.

MEDITATION 30

VAINGLORIOUSNESS

Read Numbers 13:31-33.

The word for today—*vainglorious*—is quite a mouthful, isn't it? It's a beautiful old word whose definition isn't so difficult. After all, *vain* isn't tough; most people know it means "conceited." *Vain* people—people other than ourselves, of course—spend most of their time fawning over what they see in the mirror.

Glorious could be used to describe a peacock—it's similar to *splendid* or *awesome.* To be *vainglorious,* therefore, is to take great pride in your own splendor. Who could be guilty of that?

Certainly not the scouts sent to check out the land of Canaan. Once they had given their report to Moses, telling him about the size of the warriors they'd seen, they spread out among the people and made their descriptions even more unforgettable. I love verse 33: "We seemed like grasshoppers in our own eyes, and we looked the same to them"—referring, of course, to the Nephilim.

The first line of that verse says it all: "We seemed like grasshoppers in our own eyes." There's the problem, of course. The spies were thoroughly and completely intimidated.

Now I've been told that I can be an intimidating figure. I'm 6'2" tall, and I weigh two hundred and too-many pounds. What's more, for years I've carried a sharp red scar down the side of my face—whose story I don't have time to tell you right now. I've had students tell me, years after I've taught them, that when they were in my class, I scared them spitless.

But I've got friends who are 6'6" and even taller. And let me tell you something: when you're not accustomed to looking up at people, hanging around with really big guys seems odd. I don't know if there actually is a "small-man syndrome," but I know this much: I'd rather be taller than shorter.

So were these Canaanites big enough to play in the NBA? Who knows? They probably weren't big enough to make the Israelite scouts look like insects beside them. That was exaggeration, of course—

there's no better way to make a point than to engage in a little exaggeration.

But let's give these scouts a little credit. It wasn't that long ago that the whole lot of them were slaves. They were never warriors. What's more, they lived in tents and depended entirely on the food that God gave them. If it hadn't been for the Lord's marching orders, they would have been little more than a mob.

These guys go out and see huge walls fortifying the towns of huge people. The enemy, in other words, is *formidable.* Can we really blame them for being scared? Who are they, after all, but a bunch of desert nomads, a throng of homeless, with not a cannon to their arsenal?

Certainly, the scouts are not *vainglorious,* pumped with their own strength. If anything, they're chicken, scaredy-cats, lily-livered.

Of course, if I had been there, I'd have been a Caleb or a Joshua. No doubt. I'd have believed. I'd have told the people, "Let's go in there and kick some butt." I'd have had my fist in the air.

Sure. If we really believe that we would have acted differently, then we are the *vainglorious*. The whole point of this story is not so much Caleb's bravery as the people's lack of faith.

"The people" means us. Lack of faith. We need a Savior. And when we think we don't, we are the *vainglorious*.

There are precious many people in the world, Lord, who don't know what it is like to have you as their Savior. Help us to share with others the good news that we know as members of your family: in you there is life and love. Amen.

MEDITATION 31

THE NIGHT OF GROANING

Read Numbers 14:1-10.

This is what I saw with my eyes, what I heard with my own ears.

It was night. A desert night is usually so full of stars they seem as many as the grains of sand beneath your feet. And when the moon shines like a bright disk, strange things happen to people.

My father returned from the council and sat outside our tent, his legs folded beneath him. He was speaking to my friend Ben's father. Both of them were angry, I remember. My mother kept me away, as if I weren't supposed to hear; but when she thought I was asleep, I crept out of my blankets and slid across the sand close to where they sat. I couldn't sleep. When a man's voice reaches a certain pitch, children become afraid. That pitch I heard in my father's voice. I couldn't sleep.

Everywhere there were fires. Not big and raging fires, but so many fires that I understood that no one was sleeping—everywhere in the camp mothers and fathers were awake and fearful. That's what I remember about that night. I couldn't see my father from where I lay, but I heard his voice. I looked up into the heavens that often seemed so full of stars, but that night, with all the fires around us, everyone awake, the desert sky seemed a black slate; the moon itself had withdrawn in sadness.

And the voices, though never loud, were angry. Lying on the warm sand, I thought the chorus of voices seemed pitched like a murmuring swarm of angry bees.

I listened to the sharp sounds in their voices. Once the footsteps of the neighbor had disappeared into the hum of mumbling all around us, my mother came to the front of the tent and sat beside my father. That was when my father cried.

I was only a child, but I remember it well. He cried because we had listened to Moses, because we had left Egypt, because behind us, he said, lay a life worth living—a home, not a tent; food, not manna; the great river, not miles of sand.

I listened to my father cry in a kind of anger. And then I fell asleep.

I awoke early in the morning from the sound of more angry voices. I was still outside the tent where I'd fallen asleep the night before, so I crawled back in. My parents were gone. They had not slept. No one had. Only children.

The noise from the tabernacle was loud, full of shouting, so I ran through the tents until finally I came to where the dust was rising. Voices were ringing into chants. There I saw Moses on the ground, screaming, crying—the way my father had the night before. Moses was begging the people not to rebel. I didn't know what he meant.

Caleb begged the people not to be afraid. I heard his words burning in the air. "Do not be afraid," he said, but his words died in the groaning.

And then I saw my father and Ben's father, who had sat beside him the night before, the man he'd talked with so long, the man who'd left my father in tears.

I saw him because I heard again his voice, his angry voice. I heard what he yelled at Moses, at Caleb. I saw hatred set in my father's eyes, and, gripped in his hands, one large stone.

Rebellion comes so easily to us, Lord. Help us to be confident that you're guiding us and protecting us all through our lives, that you are our God, just as you have promised. Amen.

MEDITATION 32

OBITS

Read Numbers 14:26-35.

I hope you don't think I'm weird, but I've always loved obituaries. I don't think I read them because I'm morbid or because I've got this thing about death—at least I hope not. I read them because an obit—every one of them—is really the outline of a short story; some of them, in fact, are novels as thick as something by James Michener.

A while back, we visited Washington, D.C. Every morning before the rest of the family was out of bed, I read the *Washington Post,* cover to cover, including the obits—almost every one. I didn't know the people who'd died, but I still enjoy the way an obit outlines a whole life in just a few paragraphs.

When we first moved to Iowa eighteen years ago, I remember reading a ton of obits that all seemed the same. Many of those who live in this area are descendants of Dutch immigrants who came to this country at the turn of the century. Between 1976 and 1986, many of those immigrants died. Lots of obits in the local papers would begin with a sentence like this: "Arie Vander Zanderbergen was born in Barneveld, Gelderland, the Netherlands." Today, just a few years later, such obits are rare. A whole generation of immigrants is gone.

Imagine a kid named Rebecca. At the time of the great rebellion against Moses, she is, say, fourteen, old enough to understand what happened the day her parents chickened out of taking the land God promised was theirs. Rebecca knows God's sentence for her people. She understands that this whole swarm of Israelites will wander homelessly until a whole generation is gone.

Now imagine that Rebecca, like me, is a obit reader. By the time she's twenty, she's married. When she's thirty, she has five children; and all of that time she's been reading the *Desert Gazette*, skimming over years of Isaacs and Shachmeds and Rahabs, all of them history.

Rebecca knows that her parent's generation, the ones who backed away from faith, *all must die* before she'll get a meal without sand in her sandwiches. I'm being somewhat silly here—after all, she's not going to be eagerly scratching marks onto her tent walls: we're talking about her mother and father, her grandparents, her uncles and aunts. *All* of them must die.

I once had a teacher who used to threaten us constantly. "Heads will roll," he used to say, one long finger in the air, if we didn't have our assignments finished. God himself uses language just as memorable in today's passage. "Your bodies will fall," he says twice, aiming his words at the grumbletonians.

By the time she's a grandmother—say, fifty years old—Rebecca has listened to the sound of a whole generation of bodies falling, thudding in the soft sand of the desert wilderness. She's read the obituaries of a whole generation of skeptics.

God's punishment is painful in its irony: "So you didn't think you could take Canaan?" he says. "Okay, you won't. You never will. How would you like a forty-year campout?"

But one element of their fear he reverses, lovingly, in verse 31. The children of these faithless wanderers will not be plunder to the Canaanite tribes; instead they'll be conquerors.

Think of Rebecca, at fifty, sitting on a desert rock and cutting long thin straps from the cured hide of an ox, knowing that this pair of desert hiking sandals will be the last she'll ever have to fashion.

Soon, she knows, she'll finally be home.

Lord, be with your people wherever they are wandering, whether it's in the desert or in the jungle, the city or the country, the mountains or the plains. Keep us faithful. Forgive us for our unbelief. Thank you for your promise to love us. Amen.

MEDITATION 33

REDEEMING OURSELVES

Read Numbers 14:39-45.

"The secret," Danielle thought, "is thin paint." That's why she kept the thinner beside her as she sat on her haunches painting the backyard fence. "Keep the paint thin," she told herself, "and I'll fly through this. That'll show them I'm sorry."

Racing through it was important to her because she wanted to work her tail off. What she'd done was wrong—she knew it when she took that tank top, knew it the moment the thought came to her in the dressing stall. It was just that she was so sure nobody would catch her.

She was wrong. Her parents grounded her, assigned her to paint the whole back fence on her own, a job they said ought to take ten days.

"Keep the paint thin," she told herself, "and you can finish it by Saturday." She worked from six till six, breaking only for lunch.

On Thursday night after work, her dad came outside with a brush. Her strategy was working, she figured.

* * *

Marc hadn't learned his lines. Unfortunately, he was falling in love again, this time when he could least afford it. It wasn't that he didn't want to be in the play—he did. But he hadn't sat down and gone through the hard work of memorizing his part. He didn't get to it.

That's why he got canned. That's why Ms. Bandstra told him it was over—the whole cast couldn't go slouching along for one more night with someone who didn't do his work. The practices were chaos, she said, just because Marc, the big star, didn't know his lines.

So he sat up half the night, his door closed so his mother couldn't see the light on, and he learned every last line. He was the first kid at school Wednesday morning, the first one in Bandstra's room. "Listen," he said. "I got it. Give me a line—any line at all."

Bandstra was still burned. At first, she wouldn't look at him; but when he started in right from the first page, she sat down behind her desk, wet her lips, and picked up the play book.

"I want it," he told her after ten straight minutes of recitation.

She turned the book in her hand, and nodded. Never said a word, just nodded. And Marc left, happy.

* * *

What the Israelites are up to in today's passage is really human, isn't it? The Lord God humbles them with this awful punishment for their lack of faith—banishment for forty years, the death of an entire generation—and the next moment they reach for their bootstraps, fill their rifle clips, spit on their palms, and take off for the promised land, confident that what they're doing is going to win back the Lord's favor.

Like Danielle, thinning the paint. Like Marc pounding his lines into his head. The Israelite people assume that if they work their tails off, God will love them.

It worked for Danielle, and it worked for Marc. Unfortunately, it didn't work for the Israelites.

We don't buy God's love with our sweat or our sweetness. We don't redeem ourselves by helping the homeless, by quitting smoking, or by buying the Christian school a new basketball floor.

The Israelites, confident that God will love their pluck and admire their ambition, rush headlong into horrifying defeat in Canaan. It's so sad, but it's so much—well, like us, isn't it? We love to think we can do it alone.

Only God is God. Only he redeems. That's the good news.

So often we are confident that we can do things on our own, Lord. We like to believe that we can earn your love—that if we do enough good things, you'll surely love us. But you love us anyway. We can't buy what you give us. Thank you for what you've given us in your Son. In his name, Amen.

MEDITATION 34

THE LOST GENERATION

Read Numbers 15:1-5.

On April 6, 1945, the Fourth Armored Division of the U.S. Army, on its way to meet the Russian Army, discovered a cluster of wooden huts at a place that seemed to be a checkpoint of some sort. Just inside the gate, they discovered the bodies of twenty-nine prisoners shot in the back of the neck only hours before. What they'd discovered was a concentration camp named Buchenwald.

A little further in, fifty-nine naked bodies lay covered with lime. And in a forest nearby the Americans stumbled onto huge pits that held between two and three thousand dead human beings. Imagine what two to three thousand dead bodies must look like, must smell like.

You have to appreciate what Lieutenant Colonel James van Wagenen, the commanding officer, did after he saw it. He went into the nearby town of Ohrdruf and ordered the mayor, a man named Albert Schneider, to witness for himself the pit of death his troops had stumbled upon, as well as the camp called Buchenwald.

Schneider appeared to be overwhelmed. He claimed that some people had whispered about the horror happening in the camp outside his village, but he said he couldn't believe any human beings were capable of the cold-blooded killing he saw that day.

Van Wagenen asked him to assemble the leaders of the village for another tour of the camp at Buchenwald the next morning. But for the mayor there was no next day. That night, he and his wife killed themselves.

I have before me a photo of seven people—all Germans—standing in a row and looking, the next day, upon the horror that was Buchenwald. Five of them are women. Four of those women are holding each other up. One is holding a handkerchief to her face, the others stand in silence, their arms up across their chests. Everyone squints. One mouth gapes. Across the others, lips are pulled tight as wires.

Sometimes I wonder about those people—what happened to them after the war, after they witnessed Buchenwald and Auschwitz and

Dachau, when they discovered their part in the evil that had been done.

Although Hitler had no children, imagine growing up knowing your father did what he did. Imagine growing up knowing the whole world associates your father or mother with the murder of millions of Jews. Imagine having to grow up with that immense burden.

The children of Nazi war criminals have to be a lost generation. Maybe some of them changed their names; maybe some moved away from Germany to try to escape their identity; maybe some, like Peter before Christ's enemies, simply denied knowing anything. They must be a lost generation. Imagine being the children of Mr. and Mrs. Albert Schneider and knowing their story.

After the Israelites' rebellion at the doorstep to Canaan, God Almighty creates what seems to be a lost generation. We're going to skip some passages in the next few chapters because in the Bible the forty-year punishment passes, it seems, with very little mention—only two stories and some more ceremonial laws.

We don't know what happened during those forty years, where the wandering took the people, what they ate, how they felt. It's all silence really. We don't know anything. We *do* know who died.

An entire generation was lost, really. Not *lost* as in not knowing the way. They knew the way. They knew the destination. They could see the promised land.

Lost, instead, as in perhaps much better forgotten.

Our lives are not lost, Lord. You have chosen us for service. Thank you dearly for giving us life and love and meaning. Help us serve you in ways that you make clear to us. Thank you for finding us. Amen.

MEDITATION 35

THREE SINNERS

Read Numbers 15:22-29.

"With what Cara knows about Cassie, she could write a book—no kidding! Cassie told her how one time she'd lied to her parents and told them she was staying over at Evie's in Bridgeport when really she was with Jason all night. And you know what I mean by 'with.'

"Really, almost every weekend Cassie grabs some kind of booze out of her parents' liquor cabinet, and you know what else? Her parents never get smart either. She's smoked since she was thirteen, off and on, and she used to hang out with this kid named Alex. All you had to do is look at him and you knew he was trouble.

"She doesn't study, and whenever she can she leeches assignments off Cara, comes sniveling up to her just before class. 'Cara, oh, Cara,' she says, 'what would I do without you?' And then she mooches homework. It happens almost daily—I'm not kidding. And she wears these clothes that hardly anybody else dares to be seen in. Well, you know Cassie. What am I telling you for?"

One of the most popular games for Christians in the last, say, five hundred years, is something called "Name the Sinner." No game board is required, no game pieces, and you can play it anywhere, anytime.

Let's try it with the little monologue we just read through. See those red buttons in front of you? When I say "name the sinner," the first one to hit the button gives the answer. Ready? Okay, maybe you ought to look at the passage again. Done? All right. Here we go.

In the little story above, name the sinner.

Too bad. It's a tie.

The answer is obvious, right?—Cassie. She drinks, smokes, lies, performs dirty deeds with boys who wear earrings. What's more, she's lazy and she dresses like—well, if you believe the voice in the above paragraphs, she dresses like a slut. For that matter, if you believe the voice, Cassie is a slut.

If you named Cassie, you were right. She's a sinner. But if you said Cara, you were right too. If you were really sharp and tried to put a name on the speaker, you weren't wrong either.

Cassie sins, let's say, most flamboyantly, most obviously. Cara probably sins by spreading wicked stories about her flashy sinner friend. And what about the voice behind the story? The fact is, the person who owns that voice—someone nameless—is a Cassie wannabe. She claims to be outraged, but she'd probably love to get all the attention Cassie attracts.

Some sins don't take Sherlock Holmes to identify. Let's name a few—illicit sex, too much booze, devil-worship, abortion, drugs. We could keep going.

Others are a little less dramatic—gossip, envy, anger, pride.

In fact, some of those "other" kinds of sins are so slick the way they slip into our hearts that often we don't even know they're there. That's right. I got 'em too, believe me. In fact, they're really in there permanently. They make your soul a minefield.

The point of the passage today is that God wanted offerings for *un*intentional sins—even the sins people didn't remember doing, the ones they didn't recognize, they ones they never even felt.

How on earth can we do that, really? How can we beg forgiveness for sins we don't recognize we've committed? How can we know what we did wrong when we don't know?

The answer is easy. *We* can't. We can't really do a whole lot about it. Thank the Lord that Jesus Christ is our sacrifice.

Yours, mine, Cara's, Cassie's—and all who call on him, even when we don't know what we did wrong.

For some of us at least, Lord, our very worst sins
are the ones we don't recognize in ourselves.
Open our hearts, Lord, help us to see you and
live in the light of your purity. Amen.

MEDITATION 36

HOLY TERROR

Read Numbers 15:30-36.

Now if you've "got your ears on," as truckers used to say, you might remember that just yesterday when we played "Name the Sinner," I told you it was a sin to pass judgment on Cassie, even though she smoked, drank, lied, and violated every law a good Girl Scout lives by.

In today's passage, what happens? Some poor schmuck, probably short on kindling for his family's woodstove, sneaks out to pick up what he can. The problem is, it's the Sabbath. And in the Israelite camp, people don't pick up firewood on the Sabbath. It just isn't done.

Let's really build this up. This man is the father of fourteen, and he's been unemployed since the tent company closed its doors. His wife is down with the whooping cough, and all of his children are huddling under his old army blanket, trying to chase the chill from their limbs.

Tell you what—let's make him homeless. His family has been living in a lean-to since they got evicted from the low-rent housing where they lived. The desert gets cold at night under brilliantly clear stars. The man's so desperate, he doesn't even know it's the Sabbath.

And what happens? Some holier-than-thou grabs the poor old soul and hauls him in front of Moses and Aaron. What do we do with this sinner?

Here's the bottom line: he's killed, stoned, for picking up wood on the Sabbath.

Now you explain to me how this horror could have occurred. I thought this God was fair. And after all, aren't we all sinners? My goodness, some sins are so slippery we don't even know we're doing them—unintentional sins, right?—like the ones discussed in yesterday's passage.

Where do Moses and Aaron get off, acting so high-and-mighty?

Well, read closely. Verse 34 indicates that Moses and Aaron didn't know what to do with him. It was the Lord's voice that commanded the Israelite's death, not Moses or Aaron.

But that doesn't answer the bigger question. Why *this* guy? Was picking up firewood such a horrendous crime? My word, even those

who didn't believe that God could help the Israelites whale on the Canaanite giants got off with only forty years.

What, really, do we know? We *don't* know that the guy was homeless. We don't know much at all about him. His story comes just after a passage describing what has to be done to really flagrant sinners, those who know better but poke a sharp stick in the eye of the Lord anyway. Those, the Lord tells Moses, stay guilty. They're the unforgiven.

All this blather about the poor man is something I drew around the story. We don't know any of that. It could well be that he used one of those sticks he picked up in the desert to shove into the eye of the Lord. The law and the example occur right beside each other, after all.

I wish I could explain this story reasonably. I wish I could write something here that would make you say, "Okay, Lord, I get it."

Guess what? I can't. All I know is, God is God, and I'm not. Once we start believing in him because we think he's doing things the way we would, we're in trouble. We start thinking God should act the way we want him to.

The lesson of this passage is actually quite clear, and it can be summed up in one word: *obedience*. Nobody ever claimed obedience was piece of cake.

Lord, help us to be better servants. Help us to obey you, even when voices inside of us want to rebel, go our own way, think we know better than you do. Rescue us from ourselves, Lord, and give us peace. Amen.

MEDITATION 37

A HOLY NATION

Read Numbers 16:1-3.

A few years ago, I answered phones for a television ministry. At the end of each program a telephone number flashed over the screen, and the preacher asked people to call if they wanted someone to talk to.

For a few days, I was that someone. The calls I received were often fascinating and sometimes weird. One of those calls sticks in my mind.

It's a lady's voice, and you can tell she's frantic, even though it's still well before six in the morning. Behind her, kids are bawling and grouching; you can hear them over the phone. It's a mess. The chaos comes right through the wires.

"Pray for me," she says to me. "Won't you pray for me, sir? I've got too many kids."

It's not a request I'd ever heard before, but I really can't say no, right? I mean, I'm not about to say too many kids is a dumb thing to pray for and slap down the phone. So I do—I pray for her.

You may not believe this, but it's true. Once I prayed into that phone, I heard her breathe more easily. I'm serious. "Oh, thank you, thank you, thank you," she said, as if I'm the miracle worker. Just a prayer—that's all. I just said a quick prayer into that phone.

I'm going to be honest—I didn't like it much. I have no doubt that my little telephone prayer, through copper wire or fiber optics, brought that distraught mom some comfort. But I didn't like being the holy man—if you know what I mean.

The fact is, that woman didn't need *me* to pray for her; she didn't need anybody. She could have prayed herself. But my praying for her was almost sacramental to her; it was a blessing. There's something really photogenic about the Pope raising his hands to bless thousands who gather beneath him as he stands on a balcony overlooking St. Peter Square, but I've got no desire to be him, as if I'm somehow closer to God than anybody else. I'm no holy man.

Praying with her the way I did made me feel strange because I am, for better or worse, a child of the Reformation. One of the great battle cries of that holy war was the "priesthood of all believers," the claim that the people of God didn't need certain individuals as designated pray-ers, the belief, instead, that we all need to do it ourselves. I believe that idea is even at the base of the political theory of democracy. I believe in the "priesthood of believers."

Apparently, so did Korah, Dathan, and Abiram, thousands of years before Luther and Calvin. They accuse Moses of the same crime the reformers laid on the church of their day—"We're *all* holy," they say in verse 3. "We believe in the 'priesthood of all believers.' "

I like their argument. But often the very best arguments are only half-truths. That's what makes them good lies.

Korah, Dathan, and Abiram are right, of course. Israel is, in a way, a holy nation, even though their track record isn't securing them a place in the Righteousness Hall of Fame. In God's eyes, we're *all* important. The rebels aren't wrong.

But you don't have to read far into the story to know that while their argument isn't way off the mark, their motives stink to high heaven.

Not long ago it was Aaron and Miriam. Now it's Korah, Dathan, and Abiram. But it's the same old song—rebellion. Haven't we heard this before? Guess what?—we'll hear it again—and again, and again. Sometimes the whole story seems like forty years of the same old chorus.

Lord, you have guided your people through wildernesses, through unbelief, and even though rebellion. We don't keep our promises well, Lord, but we take great hope and courage from the fact that you do. Thank you for being our Lord and Savior. In Jesus' name, Amen.

MEDITATION 38

AUTHORITY OR AUTHORITIES? (1)

Read Numbers 16:4-11.

I'm going to quote something I stumbled across when reading about the story of Korah, Dathan, and Abiram. But before I do, I want you to know this: these words were written in the fifteenth century at the time of the Reformation. Here's the passage. See if you can understand what the author is saying.

> *If, therefore, we are afraid of contending with Him [God], let us learn to remain in our right place. For, however they may prevaricate [lie], [those] who disturb the church through their ambition, in fighting against the servants of God, they attack Himself [God Almighty]. And therefore it is needful [that's an old-fashioned expression] that He [God] should resist them, to avenge Himself.*

Tough? Okay, I know it is. But there's something really fascinating here. If you didn't understand, let me paraphrase. The writer says in his own fifteenth-century way that those who fight against the church are going to get nailed by God Almighty, since God knows that those who fight against the church are really fighting against him.

Now here's what's interesting. This passage, written at the time of the Reformation, was written not by the pope or some important bishop of the Roman Catholic Church, but by John Calvin, as in "Calvin the reformer." Isn't that amazing? While he and his followers were "reforming" the church ("tearing it down," you'd say, if you were Roman Catholic at the time), Calvin rails on rebels who rail on the church!

But there's more. In his commentary on the Scripture passage for today, Calvin takes a little time out to punch at the pope. I'm not the only one to see Korah, Dathan, and Abiram's rebellion as something a whole lot like the Reformation: "How utterly ridiculous, then," Calvin writes, "is the folly of the Pope in comparing all the enemies of his tyranny to Korah, Dathan, and Abiram." The Pope drew the analogy himself, I guess.

And although this book I'm quoting from is, for the most part, just Calvin's play-by-play account of the Old Testament stories, right here—at this story—he takes time out to tell the pope that he'd like to step out into the alley for a moment and settle this whole matter.

The difference between me and Korah, Calvin says, is that Korah and his cohorts are taking shots at people who *deserve* their praise: "Who is Aaron that you should grumble against him?" Moses says in verse 11, as if to say his brother has done nothing to bring on their anger.

What's different, says Calvin, is that the priests Calvin knows are scoundrels, not saints. "In order to prove that his cause is connected with that of God [Calvin's talking about the pope now], let him show us the credentials of his calling, and at the same time thoroughly fulfill his office," something Calvin implies the pope hasn't done. In other words, Calvin thinks the pope is a scoundrel.

There's the difference, says Calvin. People who want others to respect their authority have to *earn* it. Moses and Aaron are, by their actions, God's people. Calvin says the pope can't argue that what happens in Numbers 16 is like what was happening in the sixteenth century.

So what? "Calvin and Hobbes" is better than Calvin and the pope—at least funnier. Who cares about history anyway?

Well, I do, for one. But I'm out of room. Hang in there and tomorrow I'll come back to this. Okay, maybe a roller coaster is more fun, but a passage like this is a lot more useful.

Let me try to explain.

Help us to study your Word, Lord. Help us to gain the insight we need from what you've allowed us to read in your Holy Book, so that our lives may be made easier by the truth you give to us. Help us to grow in you. Amen.

MEDITATION 39

AUTHORITY OR AUTHORITIES? (2)

Read Numbers 16:8-11.

In Europe during World War II, Christians often met in secret places to discuss whether or not to fight against the Nazis who had overrun their nations. There were two arguments: (1) Yes, we should because the Nazis' invasion and their persecution of the Jews is against God's law; (2) No, we shouldn't because God demands respect for those in authority over us. Give unto Caesar what belongs to him, after all, right? Didn't Jesus himself say that? After all, he lived under an evil occupation too. He never picked up a sword to fight.

Knowing what we know about Hitler today, that discussion doesn't seem too tough to figure out. Many of us would say the right thing to do was to fight.

When I was twenty, tons of young people opposed the war in Vietnam. Some radicals even fire-bombed government buildings, shut down traffic, and rioted on college campuses. Why? Because they were sure that sending innocent Americans to die and killing thousands of Vietnamese was wrong. They believed that the nation's leaders—President Nixon especially—were evil.

Back then I knew Christians who argued the same issue as European Christians during the second world war: when is it right to disobey the authorities God, by his will, has set up over us?

Or how about this? Millions of aborted fetuses have died since abortion has been legalized and the killing goes on. As I write this, some political leaders want the health program in the U.S. to include free abortions for poor women. They want *my* tax dollars to be used to pay for something I stand vehemently against.

In that situation, what should I do? Do I accept the authority of the authorities, or do I disobey? In other words, do I obey the government or my own conscience?

It may seem farfetched to you, but Christians have asked themselves these questions throughout our history. And even though the issues were different in the Reformation, and abortion isn't quite the same as the Vietnam War or the terrors of Nazi occupation, all three cases raise the same issue: should Christians disobey their rulers, the authorities?

That's a tough question, one that almost every generation of Christians has had to ask at least once in their lives. Some Christians ask it every day.

Now, what does Calvin say the difference is between Korah, Dathan, and Abiram—their rebellion against Moses—and Luther, Zwingli, and himself, and their rebellion against the church? After all, as I told you yesterday, the pope claimed Korah and Calvin were of the same stripe.

Calvin says one defines *authority* by the *authorities.* Moses and Aaron were appointed by God to take authority; so, Calvin would say, was the pope. But Moses and Aaron, once in office, did what the Lord wanted. That made what Korah, Dathan, and Abiram did, their rebellion, flat wrong. No question about it, according to Calvin.

If our leaders, our authorities, don't do what's right, don't deal justly with the people God puts under their authority, then, Calvin would say, those authorities don't deserve their authority. Then they may be disobeyed—they *must* be disobeyed.

If you think Christianity is something that raises the spirits, you're right. If you think faith in God is something that will win you eternal life, you're right too. If you think loving Jesus is something that gives your life meaning, you're right on target, sister.

But if you think your faith has nothing to do with this fallen world, you're dead wrong. It does. How should we live? That's been a question Christians have asked themselves for centuries—and so do we.

Give us the wisdom to know how to apply your
will and your Word to our everyday lives, Lord.
Help us know when to act and when to sit still;
when to crusade and when to be silent. Keep us
close to you. Through Jesus Christ our Lord, Amen.

MEDITATION 40

SHIBBOLETH

Read Numbers 16:12-13.

I've got the front page of an old newspaper framed and hanging from my office wall. I framed it because the graphic was something I didn't want to lose. I knew way back when that it would eventually be thought of as a symbol, a kind of relic, of the whole rebellious time in which I grew up.

You probably would recognize that graphic, even if you didn't know when or why this particular rag was published. It's a whole cluster of raised, clenched fists sprouting from a single base. When I was a kid, a raised fist was a symbol of protest.

If you really wanted to be with it at that time, you not only raised your fist, you repeated certain phrases. The one I remember best is "power to the people." So here's the whole package: buy yourself a pair of bell-bottom jeans, stick a flower in your hair, string some beads around your neck, wear a headband, raise your fist, and repeat after me: "Power to the people." Zap, you're a hippie.

"Power to the people" is what people then called a "shibboleth." The word refers to the kind of phrases we elevate to super-important status. Years later, a whole generation of kids said the word "excellent" with a certain twist of the head after *Bill and Ted's Excellent Adventure* made the word a kind of shibboleth. Say "excell-ent" in just the right voice and you're in. It's that simple. That's what a shibboleth is.

The pigs in George Orwell's *Animal Farm* employed a shibboleth to calm the anxieties of the rest of the barnyard animals: "All animals are equal, but some are more equal." All they'd have to do is say it, and uneasy bits of rebellion floating in their consciences would pass in the breeze.

The fascinating thing about Dathan and Abiram's indictment of Moses is their use of a shibboleth, a single important phrase that, ironically, Moses used first. What phrase was that? "A land flowing with milk and honey."

Look at the passage again. Dathan and Abiram use the phrase in verse 13 not to refer to Canaan, God's promised land, the place Moses had set before their eyes as God delivered them from slavery in Egypt; instead—if you can believe it—they use the phrase to refer to Egypt!

Incredible, isn't it? Suddenly, the place where they were persecuted, where they were enslaved, where they were butchered by the man-who-would-be-God, Pharaoh himself, that place is called "the land flowing with milk and honey."

You have to ask yourself if the elevator, as they say, goes to the top floor. Do these rebels have sand for brains, or what?

They're really not dumb though. The fact is, Korah, representing the religious brass, and Dathan and Abiram, representing the political kingpins, are no fools. It's a mark of their savvy that they employ this shibboleth the way they do, attempting thereby to turn people's minds into mush. "Here we are in the desert," they say, "when we could have been in the land of milk and honey." Notice this too: they never once use the word *Egypt.*

Sly foxes. But they're doomed. My word, are they doomed.

Dathan and Abiram's use of the shibboleth, like everything else that passes from their mouths about Moses and Aaron, is a flat-out lie. And they'll know it, soon enough.

This is another one of those not-so-sweet stories. Read on.

Lord, your Word is rich with life itself. In it we find
the path of salvation, but we also find so much
about life itself as we live it from day to day.
Thank you for this great wisdom book, and
help us, through this Word, to see Jesus. Amen.

MEDITATION 41

OF GOD AND FOOLS

Read Numbers 16:15-34.

Is there an echo in here?

Now let's get this straight. What we've got here is the story of a bunch of guys who want to get rid of Moses. In Act 1 they trump up some false charges, make a scene that gets everybody riled up, and then claim great credit for themselves.

Act 2. At the moment the rebellion is white-hot, God appears, and "the glory of the Lord" stops the people dead in their tracks. (I still wish I knew what the glory of the Lord looked like. Once again, it brought the house down.)

Act 3. God threatens to wipe out the whole sorry mess, but Moses, an all-around nice guy, calms the Lord down a little by telling him that destroying every last Israelite isn't good public policy.

Act 4. God listens to Moses' pleading, allows the people of Israel to live, then wipes out the anarchists by an earthquake with a monstrous appetite and an all-consuming fire created by a few holy howitzers.

I repeat: is there an echo in here? Haven't we been through this all before? Rebellious men, false accusations, one really ticked God Almighty, Moses begging for a little mercy? Have I seen this movie before or am I just suffering from terminal *déjà vu*?

Sounds like a movie classic, all right, and you only have to thumb back a few chapters to get to Miriam and Aaron, Moses' own family, who tried to pull a similar *coup d'etat;* fortunately for them, they lived to talk about it.

With any kind of memory at all, Korah, Dathan, and Abiram couldn't possibly have forgotten Nadab and Abihu, who not all that long ago lit up some unholy fires and got themselves burned in the process. In the Israelite camp, it seems, somebody's always complaining. The fact is, rebellion has been a feature of nearly every story we've read in this book.

I don't want to question God, but after a few chapters, you start to wonder why on earth he cares anymore. Moses had a vested interest here; when he begged God not to destroy Israel, he may have been thinking of his own kids.

But really, what's the point here? Why does God continue to tolerate these headstrong dolts? They no more than get thrown into forty years of aimlessness than they start in on their miserable whining again!

A good friend of mine claims no "Christian" writer could have written the Bible. He says the stories in it—especially the ones we've been reading—are really too ugly for what we call "Christian" writers. Go to your nearest Christian bookstore and see if you can find a book filled with as many distasteful stories as this Bible we've been reading. You'll be there all month.

In this book, *we*—that is, God's own chosen people—don't come off very well. We come off, in fact, like fools, demented fools at that.

There are only two themes to the whole Exodus saga, two themes that have to be spelled out in bold: **humanity's stubborn rebelliousness** and **God's overwhelmingly incredible love.** He is our God, but sometimes he has to haul us, kicking and screaming, into the comfort of his grace.

My friend may be right: no "Christian" writer would have written a book that reflects so wretchedly on believers. Only God would write this book. It has really only one basic idea: as incredible as it seems, he loves us.

We're the fools. We can't seem to get into our thick skulls the fact that we need him. But our forgetfulness doesn't change the basic shape of the story. **The good news is he loves us anyway.**

That's the whole truth, the gospel truth. So help me God.

Thank you for hanging in there with us, Lord.
Thank you for always being there. Even when
we conveniently forget you, you don't forget us.
In Jesus' name, Amen.

MEDITATION 42

INSTANT REPLAY

Read Numbers 16:36-50.

Can you believe it? Do you see what I mean about horrible stories? Listen, I'm a writer of sorts, and if I wrote story after story as downright depressing as these, my mother would likely pray daily for my writing soul. I'm not kidding.

A day after the Lord appears in a ballistic shower of pyrotechnics that ends the lives of a whole crowd of rebels, just twenty-four hours after God tells Israel to retrieve singed censers and pound out a memorial to the horror they'd witnessed firsthand, one rotation of the earth after the glory of the Lord had appeared once again to the Israelites and stopped them in their tracks, the grumbletonians are at it again: "*the next day* the whole Israelite community grumbled against Moses and Aaron (v. 41)."

Once more, the Lord tells Moses to step back while he incinerates the whole sorry bunch. Once more Moses pleads for the people, this time using Aaron's sacrifice as a buffer. And once more, thank goodness, the Lord God Almighty bridles his wrath, even though nearly fifteen thousand more people died. Way back in the days of record players, we used to say "the needle's stuck." That's exactly what happens here. We keep hearing the same tune.

And irony—talk about irony! Listen to this: just twenty-four hours before, the people who now rail on Moses and Aaron were saved precisely because Moses and Aaron begged God to save their necks—and souls.

There's more. Those same people, angered about the deaths of Korah, Dathan, and Abiram, call the rebels "the Lord's people," even though the showdown at the Tent of Meeting made it abundantly clear that the Lord God Almighty wouldn't claim them in a month of Sundays.

There's some irony all right. But for stupidity, you can't beat this: the new rebels accuse Moses of killing off the old rebels, though Moses couldn't have opened the desert earth the way it opened unless he'd had an arsenal of Tomahawk missiles or a whole fleet of earth movers.

"You shouldn't have done that, Moses," they scream, as if he'd stuck his fingers into the ground and split the earth like a ripe melon. It's plain crazy. It's nuts.

Really, could you blame God Almighty for erasing the whole sorry gang of grumbletonians? Would you say he was malicious or excessively violent if he just deleted the whole mob?

I wouldn't. Is it stupidity? Is it blindness? Is it anger about forty years of wandering? What is it with these people that makes them forever miss the point?

I don't think I understand why they don't wise up, but I know their reactions are totally human. And I know this too: if I were God, I'd probably nuke the whole works. Why not? Who needs the headache?

But the fact is—as we've said before—*I'm not God*. When I try to analyze God's way of doing things, then measure it by my own sense of right or wrong, then I'm making up a God who isn't any better than me at my best. (At best, that's an eagle scout.)

I hate to say it again, because writers know that repetition is boring and therefore death to a story. We're only halfway through the book of Numbers, but I'm going to give you the moral once again, hoping that you keep reading anyway, even though the whole truth is already out in technicolor.

Here it is: **God loves us.**

Can you believe it?

Lord, I don't know how we can ever thank you
enough for your love and care for us, your
people. It is miraculous that you care.
We live in your grace. Amen.

MEDITATION 43

DISPOSSESSED

Read Numbers 17:1-7.

Pick some major city in any country in the world. Go directly to the airport, pick up a free ticket (charge it to me), and travel there at your leisure. Once you've checked through customs, get yourself a taxi and ask the driver to take you to the most rundown part of the city. Step out of the taxi. Go on, don't be afraid. Step out. You're invisible anyway. I didn't pay for your ticket.

Now walk beneath the windows of the cluttered apartments and just listen to what the people are talking about. Tell you what, spend two hours maybe, at most, listening. Get a sense of what's happening in the community.

Okay, time's up. Chances are, you heard a lot of grumbling. It doesn't make any difference which country you chose—or even which continent. Generally, the dispossessed people of the world—the ones who "got nothing" as people say—are most interested in change, in revolution, in "getting their piece of the pie." In fact, Karl Marx built a whole view of life based on the idea that people want very badly what they don't have.

One aspect of Korah, Dathan, and Abiram's rebellion that we didn't mention yet is the fact that those three guys could hardly be called "the dispossessed." If they had been around today, Korah would be leading the biggest church in the state; Dathan and Abiram would be chauffeured back and forth to the state capitol in stretch limos. We're talking big shots here, all three of them. Heavyweights. Fat cats with extra chins.

The beginning of chapter 16 describes the rebels as two hundred fifty "elite men, well-known community leaders who had been appointed by the council." These were not the dregs at the bottom of the cultural barrel.

That fact is very important in understanding not only what happens in the rest of chapter 16, but also this strange little incident recounted in chapter 17. You see, if the rebellion had been ignited by a bunch of have-nots, it might have been over quickly. But it wasn't. These were the "elite." As a result, even though Korah, Dathan, and Abiram have been squeegeed out of the ranks, they left behind some admirers, at least some of whom held on to their heroes' own beliefs. Specifically, they believed that Moses and Aaron carried tons more weight than they were really worth.

So what was still at stake—even after death by earthquake, death by fire, death by plague—was Aaron's position as God-appointed leader of the Tent of Meeting. Some people were still questioning who's in charge.

And who sees that Aaron's position is still in jeopardy? The Lord God Almighty. Verse 1 says once more, "the Lord said to Moses. . . ."

This is an odd little chapter with an odd little miracle. In order to understand it, you have to see it in the context of the stories it follows. Even though God had terminated a whole flock of rebels, he tells Moses that something is going to have to be done to make sure his people understand that bellyaching against the servants he chooses is really bellyaching against him and his rule.

Therefore, the Lord tells Moses, gather the staffs, the symbols of power, from the heads of the tribes, and inscribe one of them with the name of Aaron.

Staffs are nothing more or less than fancy walking sticks, really. Dead sticks—long branches cut from trees. Some of them may have been decorated. I wouldn't doubt that some of the ones Moses collected were nicely carved, maybe even museum pieces.

But all of them were dead. Only God could produce almonds from a dead stick. And that, he says, is exactly what he's going to do.

Help us, Lord, like the apostle Paul, to be content in whatever situation we find ourselves. Help us to work for your good in the world, but give us the blessed gift of peace and happiness in knowing that you are our God. In Jesus' name, Amen.

MEDITATION 44

DEFEAT AND VICTORY

Read Numbers 17:8-12.

John Cheever was an interesting guy. He died a few years ago but his stories are still alive. What makes him interesting is the fact that he often seemed to see the world as Christians do, even though, as an alcoholic and a closet homosexual, he wouldn't have been highly esteemed in most churches.

But his stories testify to the way he saw life. In one of the most famous, "The Swimmer," a rich guy from the suburbs, a man who thinks he's got it made, decides to swim home through the pools that punctuate every backyard of the exclusive suburb where he lives. He starts on a kind of "good-life" marathon swim.

It doesn't work. The pools are there and so are the neighbors; but something happens to him. He hits a kind of time warp, and when he finally arrives at home, he's seen some things about himself and his world that make him terribly weary. In fact, he's almost destroyed. He slumps over at his garage door, a beaten man.

Sometimes I use that story when I teach literature. I like to tell my students that Cheever was a Christian—at least he claimed he was—although he wasn't a paradigm of righteousness. They often have trouble seeing his faith in the strangeness of his stories, but I try to explain that the way the guy in "The Swimmer" is slumped over at the end of that story, the way he sees himself at the end—as someone who had trusted in his own power and bucks—illustrates that Cheever knew there's more to life than swimming pools, no matter how beautifully emerald.

I bring that up because this odd little chapter also has an odd little ending. The Israelites complain to Moses, "We will die! We are lost, we are all lost!" The end.

That's hardly an awe-inspiring curtain, is it? If you look at the first verse of the next chapter, you'll see that suddenly we're into a whole new ball game. There's no explanation for what happened. "Are we all going to die?" the people ask. That's it. That's the end of the story.

The historic catechism with which I'm familiar, the Heidelberg Catechism, is separated into three parts: sin, salvation, and service. Those categories are not just arbitrary, really; they line up the way the Christian life "happens," if we can use that word.

Although the first part—"sin"—is the shortest, it's absolutely crucial to what follows. Why? It's easy (even though the reality is painful). We can't really say we *know* the glory of salvation—Christ's gift of forgiveness—unless we *understand* our sin. How can we know what forgiveness is if we don't know we need it?

Are you with me so far? Okay, one more thing. Recognizing sin is often very painful. We'd rather not admit it. Think of Korah, Dathan, and Abiram in those last few seconds when the glory of the Lord shut down their whole operation permanently. Can you imagine the terror that must have pierced their hearts when they recognized their own sin? They were on their knees—I'm sure.

That's it. That's the place to begin, the place where they've needed to be ever since the exodus—*on their knees.*

I don't want to be vainglorious either. On my knees is a great place for me too, even though it's a couple thousand years after Egypt. It's a good place for all of us.

It's not a pretty place or very comfortable, but what seems to be defeat can often be the first great step toward victory.

Dear Lord, please turn all our defeats into victories.
Help us to learn from whatever kinds of
experiences you place into our lives.
Help us to become more and more your
people. In Jesus' name, Amen.

MEDITATION 45

"DÉJÀ VU ALL OVER AGAIN"

Read Numbers 20:2-5; Exodus 17:1-3.

Clarice is adopted. It's not something she's bent out of shape about. In fact, she's always thought of her being adopted as kind of special. Her parents brought her up to believe that somewhere along the line some mom and dad, her birth parents, thought she was very special; that's why they gave her up to Don and Matty Gibbons—her adoptive folks.

That's not to say that she loves being adopted. She's comfortable with it, but she's conscious of it all the time, and there are moments when it seems obvious—like when she doesn't get along with her parents. When that happens, one of the first things she thinks about is that she's not really *theirs*. She knows she shouldn't think that way, but it comes naturally when she's mad—you know?

Anyway, she's in love. Nick is the guy of her dreams—good-looking, sweet, good family, romantic. Okay, she fell and fell big, but then so did he. They couldn't stay away from each other. Nothing else mattered.

One morning Clarice got so nauseous she wished she would die. The sickness went away, but it came back the next morning—and the next and the next. Soon enough she had to tell her mom what she suspected. They bought one of those little take-home tests and Clarice passed with flying colors. She was royally pregnant.

Shar is Clarice's friend, but Shar felt really shut out when Clarice fell, like totally, for Nick. I mean, she never saw Clarice anymore once they started going hot and heavy. Never—and they were best friends. So when Shar heard the news, she went over to Clarice's and sat there for a while. Clarice cried and so did she.

While Shar was driving home, this is what she thought: "That stupid, stupid Clarice. If anybody should know enough *not* to get pregnant, she should. Doggone her!—she's adopted. She knows what kind of trouble messing around can get you into."

Unfortunately, people don't always learn lessons. Take Shar. Her mom has told her a thousand times to put on her seat belt, but one day when she was driving downtown to pick up an inner tube for her little brother, a cop picked her up—twenty-five bucks down the chute.

We're all like Clarice and Shar really—every last one of us.

In Exodus 17, the first generation of grumblers complains to Moses that they've got no water. If we've heard their moaning once, we've heard it a thousand times: "Why did you haul us out to this godforsaken desert when we had it so good at home?

Now, almost forty years later, a whole new generation bellyaches with the same kind of complaint: "We got no pomegranates, Moses—and no water!" Same old song. Same old song. As Yogi Berra once said, " *Déjà vu* all over again."

Maybe if God had videotaped the whole story the first time around, they would have learned their lesson. Ah, fat chance.

Every generation, it seems, repeats the same old sins, because what all humans inherit from all human parents—in addition to eye color, hair texture, and toe length—is this predilection to sin—to complain, to bellyache, to want more.

Every month a newsletter from the town in which I live warns its residents to be very, very careful around puddles that form in the street where sump pumps gush water out of saturated yards. Algae forms, the newsletter says, and the surface can be slippery as ice.

Today, my right elbow and my right knee have apple-sized street burns because I went down on my bike—boom! Didn't listen. Figured I could make it. Didn't. My poor knee is still weeping—so am I.

Sometimes we just don't get it, I guess. But the glory is, God loves us anyway.

Thank you for your abiding faithfulness to us, your people. We try and we try, but we still fall into the same old traps, still rebel and bellyache. That you love us is miraculous—we're so thankful that you don't give up, even when we deserve it. Amen.

Don't Pray with Mud on Your Shoes is the third in a series of four devotionals on the Exodus—all by author James C. Schaap. Other titles in the series are

100% Chance of Frogs
The 40-Year Campout
Killer Snakes and Talking Mules